Ian Allan
PUBLISHING

# BUS
## BLUNDERS
### GAVIN BOOTH

First published 2009

ISBN 978 07110 3376 4

© Gavin Booth 2009

Published by Ian Allan Publishing

an imprint of Ian Allan Publishing Ltd,
Hersham, Surrey KT12 4RG
Printed in England by Ian Allan Printing Ltd,
Hersham, Surrey KT12 4RG

Code: 0907/B

Visit the Ian Allan Publishing website at
www.ianallanpublishing.com

*Title page:* If ever a bus was a blunder it was Daimler's
Roadliner, a name that crops up several times in this book.
It wasn't the Daimler part that was the problem, but the
compact Cummins V6-200 engine, here on the 1964 prototype.
It proved to be so unreliable that Daimler offered other
engines in what many believed was an otherwise excellent
chassis. If only they had stuck with a good old Gardner...

# Contents

Introduction 4

The Irish Question 5

Know Your Market 8

No Welcome in the Hillsides 11

Daimler's Big Mistake 13

Ace or Joker? 18

Some Talk of Alexander 21

Fuel Starvation 25

Bending the Rules 31

No Longer Dominant 36

Whatever Happened To... 40

National Service 43

Stick With What You Know 48

Little Things Mean a Lot 59

Municipal Muddles 67

Worth a Try 70

United is Untied 76

The Guy Who Called Wulf 78

Ahead of His Time? 83

A Deck Too Far? 85

Not Invented Here 89

How Britain Learned to Love the Integral 97

A Bridge Too Far 102

United We Fall 108

Bought Out or Sold Out? 110

Blunders in Brief 114

A London Non-Starter 117

Fair Fares Please 118

Through a Glass Darkly 119

Seeing the Wood for the Trees 121

The Sinking of Mayflower 123

Executive Decisions 126

Unpainted and Unwanted 131

Leave Your Troubles Behind 134

One Size Fits All 143

Taken for Granted? 148

A Staggering Idea 153

Inappropriate Behaviour? 156

And finally... 158

Further reading 160

# Introduction

What constitutes a bus blunder? Nobody, surely, sets out to *create* a blunder. We must assume that the busmen whose blunders are detailed in these pages set out with the best of intentions. Given what they knew at the time, they followed a reasonable course of action, the argument runs, and so they shouldn't be judged too harshly. It is, after all, often only in hindsight that we can label as blunders decisions taken in good faith.

Well, yes, we fully recognise the benefits of hindsight, but we also know there were courses of action that we recognised as blunders as soon as we learned about them – and by the same token we have been proved spectacularly wrong.

Take the ongoing efforts to find alternatives to fossil fuels, which perhaps count as blunders because they were soon abandoned and apparently came to nothing, yet engineers and operators were learning what does and doesn't work for the benefit of future developments.

Or the long-running tragedy that reduced the revered Leyland name to a national joke and which was driven by political rather than market considerations.

But then, some of us looked at the prototype Dennis Dart midibus at the 1988 show and muttered about how expensive it was and how this would deter customers considering trading up from minibuses. How wrong we were then.

And I must admit I was a bit cynical when a little Scottish company adopted the name Stagecoach, with all its cowboy connections, and stuck to the name as it grew and grew. Today when we talk about Stagecoaches, we think first about buses. Similarly when the combined Badgerline/Grampian operation was renamed FirstBus, we thought it was maybe a bit presumptuous; today, we glibly talk about 'First' – and of course it has grown to be the UK's biggest transport operator. Even the made-up 'Arriva' name for Cowie's bus and rail operations. We made jokes about Arriva-derci, but we still use the name without a second thought. No blunders there, then.

My Chambers Compact Dictionary defines a blunder as 'a foolish or thoughtless mistake, to make a blunder, to act or move about awkwardly and clumsily', and the online Wikipedia goes into the subject in greater detail:

A blunder is a spectacularly bad decision or action, a mistake or error with detrimental consequences to the party that makes it. It is typically attributable to faulty perception: the result of not reading signs, or misinterpreting available information. Naturally many sensible decisions, which even in retrospect were carefully taken, may also prove disastrous mistakes.

The term blunder is often used to refer to military, diplomatic, political, social or business decisions.

Examples of actions famously considered to be blunders include: the Japanese attack on Pearl Harbor, the Maginot Line, and The Tea Act of 1773 (and related British policy decisions toward the American colonies). However, there is often considerable debate as to whether a decision leading to failure is truly a "blunder" or merely a reasonable course of action based on the available knowledge at the time. Hindsight usually allows one to see the situation far more clearly.

A less consequential blunder is a faux pas, or a blooper.

Some of the blunders in this book may indeed be bloopers, but a 'blooperbus' is a considerably less satisfactory concept than a 'blunderbus'.

Alan Millar contributed a 'Classic Blunderbus' column to *Classic Bus* magazine for more than a dozen years. He identified bus models that could be considered Blunderbuses because they hadn't sold, because they were too advanced, because they were in the wrong place at the wrong time, and sometimes because they were simply rubbish.

Readers didn't always agree with Alan. As editor, I didn't always agree with him, but that didn't matter as it often provoked a lively debate. It is upsetting to see your favourite bus type labelled as a Blunderbus, but Alan always explained his reasoning.

Some of the buses identified as Blunderbuses have made it into this book, but it's not just the hardware that we looked at. There were company failures, ticketing systems that didn't work, companies that should have stuck with what they did best, uneasy bedfellows and grand plans that came unstuck.

What is interesting – spooky even – is the way that many of the blunders and bloopers covered in this book crop up under different headings, suggesting that an ill-thought-out bus or a badly-timed action can cause reverberations over a much wider area. Just look at the multiple mentions for the Daimler Roadliner, for example.

Of course you won't agree that all of the examples I cover can be classed as blunders as defined in your dictionary, but I include them as examples of where things didn't go quite as well as they should have done. As a Scot I can do no better than to point to the words of Robert Burns, our National Bard: 'The best laid schemes o' mice an' men gang aft a-gley…'

Gavin Booth
*Edinburgh*

# The Irish Question

Ireland's state-owned bus company, Córas Iompair Éireann, had a long history of buying British-built chassis, usually Leylands. For many years it built its own bodies on these chassis – solid, if slightly anachronistic, bodies it must be said, often built on Metal Sections frames. It bought Atlanteans and Leopards in the 1960s and 1970s and 238 Atlanteans had bodies built by Van Hool McArdle, a joint venture that took over CIE's bodyshops at Spa Road, Dublin. Van Hool McArdle also built bodies for UK operators, notably South Yorkshire PTE. Looking ahead, Van Hool built a single-deck citybus for CIE, but nothing more came of this and the joint venture foundered in 1976.

CIE became a vocal critic of Leyland products and started a conversion programme, fitting horizontal Detroit Diesel engines and Allison gearboxes into some of its Leopards, while others received DAF engines. A couple of Atlanteans received Cummins engines, but many more got DAF engines of a type that was actually based closely on the Leyland 680 family they were replacing.

CIE's dissatisfaction with Leylands was not helped by problems it apparently encountered with Atlanteans like this 1966 example – though it must be said that CIE's bodyshop came up with a very different design on Metal Sections frames.

The square-cut Germanic look of the CIE Bombardiers can be seen in this view of the 1982 prototype two-door Citybus. *Stephen Morris*

It became clear that CIE wanted to design and build its own buses, partly to create employment in Ireland but also, one suspects, as a snub to Leyland. Creating local employment is a laudable economic move but as it turned out CIE could have saved a great deal of time and heartache by swallowing its pride.

It bought no buses for a few years, squeezing extra life out of already elderly Leylands, while the German consultancy FFG created designs for a new single-deck citybus, an interurban coach and a double-deck bus. Then CIE had to find a partner prepared to build them in Ireland. After a false start with another firm, a deal was signed with the Canadian Bombardier company and General Automotive Company (GAC), and Bombardier (Ireland) was set up in 1979 to build complete buses in a factory in Shannon.

The prototype rural bus was built by FFG in Hamburg in 1983; it had a DAF engine and Allison gearbox. The KR class rural buses were possibly the most successful of the types designed for CIE.

The three prototypes, built by FFG in Hamburg, emerged between 1978 and 1980 and production started properly in 1981. The initial orders were for 50 11.1m coaches (20 for express work, 30 for touring), 120 10.4m two-door single-deck citybuses, and 200 9.6m two-door double-deckers.

Bombardier withdrew from the venture in 1983 and GAC was left as the only partner. GAC even tried to interest UK operators in the range and a rural bus was delivered to United Auto in 1985.

GAC withdrew in 1985 and the Shannon plant closed the following year.

The plant had delivered 365 double-deckers, 20 intercity coaches, 31 tour coaches, 201 single-deck citybuses, and 224 rural buses. The last buses were finished by CIE after GAC's departure.

The single-deckers were not unattractive buses, albeit rather square and Germanic with barrel-shaped windscreens. The double-deckers were rather ungainly, looking for all the world like single-deckers with an extra deck tacked on.

In the 1987 split of CIE into two bus companies and a rail company, the Bombardiers and GACs ended up with Dublin Bus (which received most of the double-deckers and the citybuses) and Bus Éireann (which received the coaches and the rural buses).

But all was not well. As Cyril McIntyre remarks in his book *CIE Buses 1945-1987*: 'Within a few years it became apparent that one set of problems had simply been replaced by another and that the latest attempt to develop an indigenous bus building industry in Ireland would eventually go the way of its predecessors.'

Initially, it seems, the new buses helped to improve vehicle availability and reduce maintenance costs, but the Irish roads played havoc with the integral body structure, particularly affecting the double-deckers, and fuel consumption was poor. After the Shannon debacle CIE invited tenders on the open market and actually returned to Leyland, building up a large fleet of Leyland and Volvo Olympians.

Many of the Shannon-built buses had relatively short lives and it is tempting to suggest that CIE would have been much better off if it had looked to models like the Olympian and Volvo B10M, both models that were on the market from the early 1980s and developing a reputation for reliability.

## BOMBARDIER/GAC PRODUCTION

| | | |
|---|---|---|
| GMDD double-deckers | 365 built | 1981-83 |
| GMIC intercity coaches | 20 built | 1981/82 |
| GMTC touring coaches | 31 built | 1981 |
| CB single-deck citybuses | 201 built | 1982-87 |
| RB rural buses | 224 built | 1985-87* |

*\* One built for export to United Auto, later bought by Bus Éireann*

### Prototypes built by FFG

| | |
|---|---|
| 1 53-seat dual-purpose bus | (1979) |
| 1 double-decker, | (1981) |
| 1 single-deck citybus | (1981) |
| 1 minibus | (1981) |
| 2 school buses | (1983/84) |

The Bombardier/GAC double-decker was a rather ungainly beast, looking like a single-decker with an extra deck added.

# Know Your Market

For European bus manufacturers, the UK represented a potentially good market. In the 1970s and 1980s DAF, Scania and Volvo had managed to gain a foothold, often at the expense of Leyland, by offering right-hand drive versions of existing models and in the case of Scania and Volvo by producing models that took the peculiarities of the UK market into account – in other words, double-deckers.

Other major builders were watching closely to identify a gap in the market. Renault, for example, collaborated with Northern Counties to introduce its PR100 model into the UK in 1988. The PR100 had already been built in right-hand drive form for Australia, and so the underframe existed; the Northern Counties body was built to Renault design.

It was not a new model as it had been introduced as the Berliet PR100 in 1972 when that company was owned by Citroën. Berliet's great rival Saviem, owned by Renault, was producing the successful front-engined SC10, but the PR100 was a rear-engined bus similar to most other European products. In 1976 Citroën sold Berliet to Renault and in 1980 Renault merged Berliet and Saviem into a new subsidiary, Renault Véhicules Industriels.

Just five UK versions of the PR100 were built – a demonstrator, one for London Buses and three for Luton Airport. The demonstrator and the London bus were quickly sold on to independents.

Renault had greater success with smaller buses in Britain. The 50-series, assembled at Chrysler's Dunstable plant, was chosen by several larger operators as a minibus chassis in the 1980s, badged initially as a Dodge and later as a Renault. The bigger S75 also enjoyed some success, but the end of production of the 50-series in 1993 brought Renault's UK bus involvement to an end.

Renault returned to the UK bus market indirectly in 2003 with the Irisbus Agora Line low-floor citybus. Irisbus had been formed in 1999 through the merger of the bus and

A Renault PR100 completed by Northern Counties, seen in 1989 working for London Buses at Chigwell Row.
*David Stuttard*

The dramatic appearance of the solitary Iveco TurboCity 100 combined the standard Iveco front end rather uneasily with the Alexander R type body. *Gavin Booth*

coach divisions of Fiat, Iveco and Renault and the Agora Line was designed by Renault and built in France. Some 20 were sold into the UK market with bodywork completed by Optare, although in total over 11,000 members of the Agora family had been built between 1996 and 2006. Since 2001, Irisbus has been 100 per cent owned by Fiat-Iveco.

Iveco also dipped a toe in the UK bus market with its rear-engined TurboCity model in 1991. This was a successful model in the Italian market, in single-deck form; the first UK TurboCity was a double-decker, launched as the TurboCity 100 – the 100 represented the target passenger capacity. In fact it managed 97, 83 of them seated, and axle weight problems resulted in a strange rear lower deck layout. It was big, at 10.7m long, and heavy, at 10820kg, and carried a variation of the Alexander R type body, married to the standard Iveco standard front end, which gave it a rather awkward appearance.

There was no rush to buy the TurboCity 100, and for a while it looked as if nobody even wanted the prototype, as it sat on a dealer's list for some time before it found a buyer. It was eventually sold and moved around various smaller independents.

In 1993 the single-deck TurboCity50 was introduced to the UK and while it fared better, it can hardly have covered its development costs. The first one carried a version of the Alexander PS type body, and six more received Wadham Stringer bodies and found homes with independent operators in England and Wales in 1994/95.

Undeterred, Iveco introduced a bus version of its successful step-entrance EuroRider coach chassis in the UK in 1997, just as operators were moving to low-floor buses, and three were bodied by Marshall; two were used by St John's Ambulance and the third went to a Scottish independent.

Although it has been unsuccessful in the big bus market in the UK, Iveco has had success here with its DailyBus minibus and EuroRider coach chassis. The blunders were not the buses themselves, which enjoyed considerable success in their own home markets, but perhaps a lack of understanding of exactly what UK operators were looking for.

## UK SALES FIGURES

| | |
|---|---|
| Renault PR100 | 5 |
| Iveco TurboCity 100 | 1 |
| Iveco TurboCity50 | 7 |
| Iveco EuroRider bus | 3 |

*Above:* Undaunted by the lack of interest in the TurboCity 100 double-decker, in 1993 Iveco introduced the TurboCity50, again with an Alexander body, in this case a two-door variant of its PS type. It was claimed to be the first bus in the UK to be fitted with a particulate filter.

*Below:* Iveco bounced back with the EuroRider, a successful coach chassis that proved less so as a bus. Three were built with Marshall bodies.

# No Welcome in the Hillsides

The highest-profile demise following bus deregulation in 1986 was the National Welsh company. It had been created by the National Bus Company in 1978 to merge two long-established bus companies, Red & White and Western Welsh, and in the NBC privatisation it was sold to its management team in 1987. So far, so good.

Like so many other former NBC companies now in the hands of their managers it decided that expansion by aggressive competition and acquisition was the way to survive. After all, wasn't this why the Conservative government had deregulated bus services? It mopped up the

Taff-Ely district council operation in 1988, then Inter Valley Link the following year, and effectively put Merthyr Tydfil Transport out of business by offering jobs to MTT drivers, also in 1989. All textbook deregulation stuff, except that the South Wales area attracted a number of smaller operators who gave National Welsh a run for its money.

Like many other NBC companies sold to their managers, after the initial excitement of controlling your own buses had

In happier days as part of the National Bus Company, a National Welsh Leyland/ECW Olympian at Port Talbot with offside Welsh-language fleetname. *S. K. Miles*

passed, the reality of running buses hit hard. The centrally controlled state-owned NBC may have frustrated managers, but they were working in the rather artificial world of regulation and near-monopoly. Revenue from operating buses in the regulated world could be fairly accurately forecast; in the brave new competitive world, nothing was certain.

Some former NBC managers recognised this early and decided to throw in with one of the large groups that were starting to emerge after privatisation. Others, like National Welsh, battled on.

National Welsh bought itself some time by selling its eastern operations, trading as Red & White, to Western Travel, which owned the adjacent Cheltenham & Gloucester bus company.

But that wasn't enough. In 1992 the receivers were called in, quickly selling off parcels of the company's operation.

Aberdare, Merthyr and Porth depots were sold, and Bridgend was closed, but by this time the vultures were moving in to pick over National Welsh's remains. Operators of all sizes and backgrounds moved in to pick up the pieces, and a plan to continue operating out of Barry depot failed.

National Welsh had simply disappeared. There would be many changes of ownership among its successors over the years and the eastern part of South Wales continues to attract competitors, even though Cardiff Bus, First and Stagecoach now cover much of its territory.

There were many other casualties of deregulation, most among new entrants to the market or coach operators that had decided to branch out, but National Welsh has been the biggest and saddest loss of a once-powerful territorial operation.

National Welsh was sold to its management in 1987, the year this photo was taken outside Barry depot showing a newly delivered Sherpa/Carlyle Bustler minibus. *Michael J. Collins*

In the very Welsh red/white/green livery of the privatised National Welsh, a convertible open-top Bristol VRT/ECW at Cardiff bus station. *G. S. O'Brien*

# Daimler's Big Mistake

You could always trust Daimler to produce good buses. Solid, reliable buses, many with Gardner engines and most with driver-friendly epicyclic gearboxes. The company never seemed to put a foot wrong. Until the Roadliner came along, that is.

Daimler was best known for its double-deckers, usually supplied to municipal operators. It had built underfloor-engined single-deckers in the 1950s, but these were heavy and rather over-engineered at a time when fleets needed lighter and more fuel-efficient chassis. When 36ft-long buses were legalised in 1961 market leaders AEC and Leyland responded with lengthened versions of their underfloor-engined Reliance and Leopard chassis, while Bristol and Daimler decided that the future lay in rear-engined types. But while Bristol got it right with its Gardner-engined RE model, poor Daimler got it spectacularly wrong with its Roadliner.

It could have been a great chassis, but for one fatal flaw: the engine. Not the obvious choice, the Gardner 6HLW, but a V6 unit from the American manufacturer, Cummins. Although today Cummins engines are popular choices fitted to a significant proportion of Alexander Dennis and Optare models, in 1964 they were little known in the UK. The V6-200 was a new and relatively untried engine. The compact nature of this vee-form engine, which was mounted in-line with the chassis, undoubtedly convinced Daimler to choose this rather than the bulkier Gardner. It was a 9.6-litre

On the surface the Daimler Roadliner with Marshall body represented an attractive package. This Potteries example is seen in Banbury on a 100-mile road test which produced an excellent fuel consumption figure of 12.2mpg – and presumably none of the problems that would dog this chassis.

## DAIMLER ROADLINER

### UK customers

**SRC6 bus**

| | |
|---|---|
| Potteries | 51 |
| Belfast | 18 |
| Darlington | 12 |
| Bournemouth | 11 |
| Chesterfield | 10 |
| West Riding | 10 |
| Wolverhampton | 6 |
| Eastbourne | 3 |
| Sunderland | 3 |
| Demonstrators | 2 |
| AA | 1 |
| Road Research Laboratory | 1 |
| *TOTAL* | **128** |

**SRC6 coach**

| | |
|---|---|
| Black & White | 18 |
| Potteries | 3 |
| Woburn | 2 |
| Central | 1 |
| Demonstrator | 1 |
| Red House | 1 |
| Tailby & George | 1 |
| *TOTAL* | **27** |

**SRP8 bus**

| | |
|---|---|
| Potteries | 10 |

**SRP8 coach**

| | |
|---|---|
| Black & White | 20 |
| Best | 1 |
| Ikzani | 1 |
| Sims | 1 |
| *TOTAL* | **23** |

### Exports

**SRC6 bus**

| | |
|---|---|
| Australia | 37 |
| Canada | 31 |
| South Africa | 31 |
| Belgium | 4 |
| Demonstrator | 1 |
| *TOTAL* | **104** |

**SRC6 coach**

| | |
|---|---|
| Canada | 3 |
| South Africa | 2 |
| Switzerland | 2 |
| Poland | 1 |
| Spain | 1 |
| *TOTAL* | **9** |

**SRL8 bus**

| | |
|---|---|
| South Africa | 27 |

192bhp unit, coupled to a Daimatic gearbox, and another advanced feature of the Roadliner was the adoption of air suspension, well ahead of most bus chassis.

A prototype chassis had been shown in 1962 with a horizontal version of Daimler's own CD6 engine, the SRD6, but no more was heard of this version, which was perhaps a pity as photos show that it would have had a completely flat floor, and so could have been ahead of its time.

The Roadliner SRC6 (Single-deck, Rear-engined, Cummins, 6-cylinder) was launched in a blaze of publicity at the 1964 Commercial Motor Show. The launch vehicles were a Marshall-bodied bus for Potteries, and a Duple-bodied coach, for Daimler saw this as a model that would be equally at home on local bus or long-distance coaching work. The portents were good and there was much interest in the Roadliner. At the same show, AEC and Leyland had introduced their new rear-engined single-deck bus chassis, the Swift and Panther ranges, and so suddenly there were three chassis to this layout on the market and competing for orders; the Bristol RE was still only available to state-owned companies.

Although Daimler won some impressive initial orders for the Roadliner and it was well received by drivers, including road-testers for the trade press, it wasn't long before rumours about its reliability started to circulate. The problem, it appeared, was the engine. There were reports of engines tightening up when hot and of excessive smoke emission.

The Daimler business had passed in 1960 to Jaguar, and in 1966 Jaguar had merged with the British Motor Corporation to create British Motor Holdings, which in turn merged with Leyland and Rover in 1968 to form British Leyland. So while AEC, Daimler and Leyland were under common ownership, there was still competition for orders and little sign of rationalisation. AEC chassis still had AEC engines, Leyland chassis had Leyland engines – but Daimler lacked its own in-house engine, and following its problems with the Cummins V6-200 turned to another proprietary engine manufacturer as an option. Perkins had a long history of building engines for commercial vehicles and its engines had been fitted to many smaller buses and coaches. Daimler chose the 8.36-litre V8.510 unit and the resulting 1968 model was the Roadliner SRP8.

This was fairly successful, and in a last-ditch attempt to salvage the Roadliner, Daimler announced in 1969 that a third engine would be tried in the chassis – the new AEC-designed 12.1-litre British Leyland V8. But the Roadliner SRL8 was built only for Pretoria, South Africa, and British Leyland was moving towards greater rationalisation. The Roadliner was dropped from the lists as the Swift and Panther would soon be in the all-conquering wake of the Leyland National.

The Roadliner was not Daimler's last single-deck chassis, though. The Fleetline was a highly successful double-deck model through the 1960s and 1970s and it seemed to make sense to adapt it for single-deck use. The 1968-introduced Fleetline SRG6 enjoyed some success; Daimler promoted the benefits of standardisation, featuring fleets that had both single-deck and double-deck Fleetlines, but in truth it was heavy with a substantial engine compartment taking up valuable body space; the Roadliner and its contemporaries had engines mounted under the floor at the rear.

In its later years Roadliner orders were cancelled by operators that had already experienced the model – nine SRP8 for Potteries, 12 SRC6 for Darlington and 10 for Johannesburg.

Cummins seemed happy to forget the Roadliner's problems when it exhibited a preserved Wolverhampton example at the 2008 Euro Bus Expo show at Birmingham's NEC, to celebrate 40 years of supplying engines into the UK bus market.

Daimler itself was on the way out, gradually disappearing under the all-conquering Leyland, but in its long and distinguished history the Roadliner was really the only blip.

*Above left:* The 1962 Daimler rear-engined prototype SRD6 chassis with Daimler's own 8.6-litre engine. Gardner engines would also have been offered.

*Above:* The 1964 Roadliner chassis was rather different, notably the bulk of the V6-200 engine at the rear.

*Left:* The root of the problem – the Cummins V6-200 engine fitted to Roadliner prototype 6000 EH.

Above: Poor old West Riding. Not only did it back a loser with the Guy Wulfrunian, it also invested in the Daimler Roadliner. This Plaxton-bodied example is seen in Wakefield bus station. *T. K. Brookes*

Below: Daimler was proud of its export orders for the Roadliner. This was one of the first, a Duple-bodied 44-seater for Edmonton, Canada, seen at the 1964 Commercial Motor

Daimler enthusiastically promoted the Roadliner throughout its lifespan, and as late as 1968 was still claiming that it was 'the world's most balanced single deck chassis', though by that time a queue of unhappy operators could well have strongly disagreed. By 1968 the Cummins engine had been dropped and operators were being offered a choice of Perkins or Leyland V8s.

# If you're looking for a low framed chassis

# Roadliner has it ready made

### Read what the press says about the Roadliner chassis and other features of this modern vehicle

'Passenger Transport' Roadliner Bus Road Test, July 1967.
"I thought the vehicle had a very nicely balanced appearance, outside and inside, and the low single step (only 15 ins above road level) and gently ramped platform represent a great advance over the older underfloor-engine types, particularly for service bus operation".
Rubber Suspension: "At full load the rubber suspension was also excellent, providing a very comfortable and quiet ride throughout the bus and excellent roll resistance in fast cornering".

'Bus and Coach' Roadliner Bus Road Test, July 1967.
Performance: "Acceleration from rest to 30 m.p.h. in 18.6 sec. is a good performance for a vehicle with a power-to-weight ratio of 11.5 b.h.p. per ton. The fact that 3rd gear gives a maximum of 30.7 m.p.h. partly explains this, as full use can be made of the available power as this speed is approached. This is an important merit, especially in urban areas".

**Daimler Roadliner, the world's most balanced single deck chassis**

**Daimler**

DAIMLER TRANSPORT VEHICLES LIMITED, G.P.O. BOX 29, COVENTRY, ENGLAND. TELEPHONE 27626 (15 lines)

Bygones are bygones, perhaps, as Cummins showed a suitably decorated preserved Wolverhampton Daimler Roadliner/Strachans at the 2008 Euro Bus Expo.
*Gavin Booth*

# Ace or Joker?

It's how everybody else started. You build a few chassis and hope that they'll prove so successful that orders will pour in and your future as a bus builder is assured. After all, AEC, Bristol, Daimler, Dennis, Leyland, Scania and Volvo all had to start somewhere.

This may be what has prompted various companies in the past 60 years to try their hand in the bus market. Few, it must be said, enjoyed much success. Even Dennis, today a name seen throughout the UK, suffered a few knock-backs until it got its bus product right. And when it did, there was no stopping it.

There have been operators who, perhaps frustrated that manufacturers were not building exactly what they wanted, decided to try it themselves. Rowe is mentioned elsewhere in this book, and more recently the Ward Brothers of Huddersfield have played their part in keeping the idea of home-made buses alive.

Ward Brothers liked Seddon Pennine coaches with Perkins V8 engines, not a popular choice, it must be said.

One of the six Ward Dalesman GRXI with Wadham Stringer Vanguard bodies built for Darlington Transport in 1983.

Seddon had stopped building what Ward wanted so the company decided to build its own chassis. An 11m prototype, model C11-640, was built for Ward's own fleet, featuring its beloved Perkins V8 plus a ZF six-speed synchromesh gearbox and bodied by Plaxton, in 1991. In 1983/84 11 of a 12m version, the C12-640, were produced and bodied by Plaxton or Van Hool for independent operators.

Ward was then persuaded to build another Seddon look-alike, the GRXI, which was similar to Seddon's RU rear-engined bus chassis. Darlington Transport bought the only six examples. In total 18 chassis had been built between 1980 and 1984, when the Ward Motors business closed, though Ward continued as a coach operator.

It wasn't long before another Huddersfield coach operator, Stephen Ives, with two of the Ward brothers, created AEC – the Albion Equipment Company. Leyland, not surprisingly, was unhappy about the use of the AEC initials and Albion name, so the company quickly became ACE – Alternative Chassis Engineering, and announced its Predator range of chassis. There was the mid-engined Puma midicoach, the Cheetah which was a Dalesman successor, and the Cougar, a rear-engined 10m bus chassis. Some 13 were sold in total and production closed in 1992.

Quest 80 was a Telford-based manufacturer that built rear-engined bus and coach chassis for UK operators between 1982 and 1987. These had Ford engines, axles and gearboxes and were bodied as buses or coaches for a variety of operators. Although the company closed in 1985 when some 50-plus chassis appear to have been built, some for export to Cyprus and South Africa, pre-built chassis continued to appear until 1987 fitted with Jonckheere coach bodies. The biggest order came from Excelsior of Bournemouth which ordered 20 VM models with Plaxton coach bodies; only 17 were delivered. In 1984/85 Merseyside PTE took delivery of six Quest B with ungainly Locomotors bodies.

Quest was taken over by Locomotors' parent, United Engineering Industries, and it was announced that Quest would build a lightweight double-decker, but this never materialised.

It must be the Yorkshire air, but in 1995 the prototype KIRN Mogul was built at Scissett in West Yorkshire. The name comes from the first initials of four entrepreneurs – the K is for Keith Ward – who saw a market for rugged

The unsuccessful Quest 80s for Merseyside Transport in 1984/85 can hardly have been helped by the weird-looking Locomotors bodies. *L. J. Long*

chassis for export markets. The hand-built 11.7m-long prototype was destined to be the only KIRN and passed into the Yorkshire Traction fleet in 2001. The Mogul had the right elements – rear-mounted Cummins C-series engine, Allison automatic gearbox – but as other manufacturers from Europe have discovered, these alone don't guarantee success.

The time and effort that goes into chassis like these probably mean that it would have been cheaper to buy a new bus off the peg. But you have to admire the determination and optimism of the men – and it is usually men – who decide to build their own buses. Everyone has to start somewhere…

**UK MARKET DELIVERIES**

| | |
|---|---|
| ACE | 13 |
| KIRN | 1 |
| Quest 80 | 42 |
| Ward | 18 |

Alternative Chassis Engineering promoted its Predator range professionally, but to little effect.

Quest 80 publicised its Model D with this brochure, and although it shows a not unattractive midibus, sales of all models stayed at 42.

# Some Talk of Alexander

Even the best bodybuilders don't always get it right. Take W. Alexander & Sons Ltd, for instance. The Alexander family started running buses in central Scotland in 1913 and by 1924 had sufficient faith in the future that a limited company was formed in 1924 and started building bodies for its own buses the same year. From 1929 W. Alexander became part of the SMT company, reformed with railway company investment, and from that time its growth was phenomenal, a shrewd mix of expansion and acquisition that was not unlike the growth of Stagecoach 60 years later. As the Alexander bus company grew to cover a territory stretching from Glasgow to Inverness, so the bodybuilding department grew and was soon supplying other SMT Group companies.

Fast forward 20 years and the sale of the SMT Group into state ownership under the British Transport Commission. The Alexander family retained the coachbuilding business, which became Walter Alexander & Co (Coachbuilders) Ltd, and gradually it expanded its customer base so that by the 1960s it could truly be regarded as a major UK supplier, and as its rivals fell by the wayside one by one it moved into the top position.

For some time its body styles were largely dictated by its principal customers in Scotland, but as its customer base broadened, its range increased and some iconic designs emerged from the Falkirk coachworks, including the legendary Y type, which was on the market for more than

Some of the earlier Alexander P types for Northern Scottish were mounted on high-built Dennis Lancet chassis, which served only to accentuate the rather square and unforgiving look of the body.

# WALTER ALEXANDER'S NEW RANGE OF STAGE-CARRIAGE BUSES

**Artist's Pre-release Impression**
**The new 'P' type Service Bus. Available**
**for 1983 delivery.**

**Robust Light Aluminium Alloy structure with a design and specification honed and tailored to meet the operators requirements for the eighties.**

*Above:* The pre-release artist's impression of the Alexander P type body was rather different from the eventual production bodies, as is often the case.

*Below:* Later P types got a partial facelift which helped the appearance, as did the lower build that was possible on the Volvo B10M chassis, here for Badgerline. *M. S. Curtis*

20 years and appeared in a wide range of variations on an equally wide range of chassis.

When it was time to retire the Y type there was great interest to see what its replacement would be. When the P type appeared in 1983 it was greeted with surprise and disappointment. Alexander had developed a thriving export business with its double-deck range and was looking to break into other overseas markets with its new single-decker. Its double-deck exports were a mix of built-up buses that were shipped complete, usually to the Far East, and kits that could be assembled locally. The kits took advantage of cheaper local labour and often satisfied a political requirement that the work should be done locally to help the economy.

The P type was designed against this background and was unashamedly square, using only flat glass in place of more expensive curved glass. As a result the sides were flat with a very shallow roof, and the front end featured a flat windscreen with a deep quarter-light ahead of the front entrance and a triangular window to the right of the driver. Pretty it was not, but it sold in small numbers – to UK operators.

Between 1983 and 1988 Scottish Bus Group, National Bus Company, West Midlands PTE and two English municipals took delivery of 72 P types, most on Leyland Tiger or Volvo B10M chassis, at a time when new big bus sales had virtually hit rock bottom. Although potential overseas sales had influenced the construction and look of the P type, none were exported.

Interestingly, when export orders came in, from Singapore Bus Service in 1988, they were for an improved version with curved windscreens and a less stark appearance. The first examples of the new PS type (the S standing for Singapore) were actually delivered within the UK, to Derby City Transport, and most deliveries over the next decade would be to UK operators, notably Mainline and Stagecoach. On Volvo B10M chassis, the PS type became Stagecoach's standard single-deck bus model before the switch to low-floor designs, and hundreds were built; the B10M/PS type was in essence Stagecoach's updated version of SBG's beloved Leopard/Y type.

So from the essentially flawed P type concept the PS type came along and showed how a rounded front and

The prototype Alexander Dash body had a shallow roof and prominent destination display, but this styling was abandoned before production began.

wider-spaced window pillars could transform an ugly duckling into a very successful swan (see page 127).

Alexander very nearly made the same mistake again when it was developing its bodywork for the Dennis Dart and Volvo B6, the new midi-size chassis that were suddenly what every operator seemed to want. A prototype body was built with a very shallow roofline, which meant that any destination displays jutted well above the roof. It is said that this was shown to Stagecoach, a major potential customer, who asked for the bus to be restyled to avoid the strange appearance of the roof. It was, and the Alexander Dash body went on to enjoy some success, though it never achieved the success of its great rival, Plaxton's Pointer.

## ALEXANDER P TYPE DELIVERIES

| | | | |
|---|---|---|---|
| Northern Scottish | 14 | Leyland Tiger | 1983/84 |
| Northern Scottish | 5 | Dennis Lancet | 1984 |
| East Midland | 9 | Leyland Tiger | 1985 |
| East Midland | 1 | Leyland Leopard re-body | 1985 |
| West Midlands PTE | 6 | Volvo B10M | 1986 |
| Fife Scottish | 13 | Leyland Tiger | 1986/87 |
| Badgerline | 14 | Volvo B10M | 1987 |
| Grimsby-Cleethorpes | 4 | Leyland Tiger | 1987 |
| Burnley & Pendle | 6 | Volvo B10M | 1988 |
| Derby | 6 | Scania K92CRB* | 1988 |

\* Although classed as P types, these were in fact PS types

The finished Dash body followed a more conventional shape.
This is one of a large order for Stagecoach on Volvo B6 chassis.

# Fuel Starvation

It took the Arab-Israeli war in 1973, the Arab embargo on oil supplies and the consequent increase in fuel prices to alert the world to the importance of fossil fuel to the world economy. This persuaded bus manufacturers and operators to look at alternative power sources and from the mid-1970s there was a spate of these, though none led to a wholesale move away from diesel as the primary fuel for buses.

There were gas buses. In 1976 Teesside Municipal Transport introduced its 'Clean Air Bus', a Daimler Fleetline fitted with a Rolls-Royce engine converted to run in liquefied petroleum gas (LPG). South Yorkshire PTE fitted a Rolls-Royce B81G gas engine to a Leyland Atlantean in 1979, and in 1980 a Ribble Atlantean entered service with a special Leyland 680LPG engine in a joint Leyland/NBC experiment.

The results of these tests were not encouraging. After over 100,000 miles in service the Cleveland bus was shown to be averaging just 3.42mpg, and the Ribble bus achieved 3.6mpg, under half of the fuel consumption of a diesel Atlantean.

Then there were electric buses. In 1972 the Department of Trade & Industry sponsored a major trial of experimental battery buses, using a BLMC 900FG truck chassis converted by Crompton Electricars and bodied by Willowbrook.

Selnec PTE took the idea further with its Seddon/Chloride Silent Rider, a full-size bus designed to operate at peak hours and recharge its batteries in between, and a Seddon/Lucas midibus.

In 1975 NBC converted a Ribble Leyland National to battery power, hauling a trailer that contained Chloride batteries. Although it was allocated to the Runcorn Busway, it spent much of its life parked up in the depot.

These well-meant experiments came to nothing and the world went back to diesel buses.

Teesside's 'Clean Air Bus' is refuelled from a Calor tanker – though the caption to the Rolls-Royce 1973 photo tells us that 're-fuelling … will not always be like this as Teesside Municipal Transport have their own liquid propane gas installation'. The bus is a Northern Counties-bodied Daimler Fleetline.

*Above:* One of the Crompton Electricars/ Willowbrook battery buses working in Doncaster for South Yorkshire PTE in 1976. *M. Fowler*

*Right:* Claimed by Chloride as 'Britain's first battery-powered bus', the Silent Rider was developed with Selnec PTE and based on a Seddon RU. A range of 40 miles was claimed and a top speed of 40mph.

The problem with electric buses was the size and weight of the batteries. One solution was to put them in a trailer towed behind a Ribble Leyland National and tested on the Runcorn Busway.

There were even suggestions in the 1970s that trolley-buses could reappear. First-generation British trolley-buses had last operated in Bradford in 1972, and over the years West Yorkshire PTE produced various drawings of a new-generation trolleybus. Although nothing came of these, in 2007 it was announced that, following the government's 2005 refusal to back the Leeds Supertram project, plans to introduce trolleybuses into Leeds had been given the go-ahead by the Regional Transport Board, subject to Department for Transport approval.

Before this, South Yorkshire PTE had gone to the trouble of buying a Dennis Dominator/Alexander trolleybus, based on its standard double-deck purchase, and erected overhead near Doncaster racecourse to test it, but it ended up at the trolleybus museum at Sandtoft.

LPG was back in the news in the late-1990s when Arriva trailed DAF/Plaxton buses at some of its companies and First and Travel West Midlands operated LPG Volvo B10Ls. Dennis Darts fuelled by CNG, compressed natural gas, were tried by Arriva Merseyside, First Bristol and Southampton Citybus, and in Optare MetroRiders by Reading Buses.

And there were battery-powered buses too– MetroRiders at Oxford, Strathclyde PTE's Omnis, which never turned a wheel in service, and the more successful Italian Tecnobuses, which operated in Bristol and on Merseyside. But again there hasn't been a rush to buy more, because battery-powered buses have suffered from heavy batteries and limited range.

The makers of diesel engines had to clean up their act and clean up their engines. Successive Euro standards have seen increasingly 'green' engines fitted to new buses and a significant reduction in air pollution.

But world events in the 21st century have prompted a fresh look at alternatives to oil, and there has been great interest in hybrid buses. There had been hybrid experiments in the late 1990s with a converted Mercedes 709D with First Provincial and a couple of purpose-built Iveco Dailys for operation in Devon, but from the mid-2000s the pace quickened.

Wrightbus developed its turbine-powered Electrocity in 2002 and this was further developed with buses entering service in London.

Stagecoach imported a Designline Olymbus from New Zealand in 2003, and further examples went into service in Newcastle and Gateshead in 2004. The Olymbus is powered by electric motors which are fed by batteries charged by a diesel-fuelled turbine.

Then Transport for London joined a Europe-wide experiment with three Mercedes-Benz Citaro hydrogen fuel-cell buses, which were operated on a three-year trial from 2004 by First London. When the trial finished in 2007 it was announced that the manufacturers had learned much from the trial and would develop more efficient buses with a greater range. Transport for London said it had plans to order 10 more, though it was generally accepted that it would be some years before fuel-cell buses would be commercially viable.

But it was widely recognised that the important developments in the near future would involve hybrid buses, and at least Alexander Dennis, Optare, Volvo and Wrightbus were working to produce such buses, very much with London orders in mind. Ken Livingstone, who was then London's mayor, said in 2006 that he wanted every new bus from 2012 to be a hybrid and his aim was to put 500 hybrid buses on London's streets each year. 'We take very seriously our role in cutting $CO_2$ emissions and tackling climate change,' said Peter Hendy, London's transport commissioner, at the time. 'We are sending a clear message to London and the transport industry that we are serious about this.'

The message clearly got through to manufacturers and it seems that after false starts with LPG, CNG, battery and even fuel-cell buses, hybrid buses will present the first real alternative to diesel buses since diesels became widespread in Britain in the 1930s.

*Above:* West Yorkshire PTE mocked up this trolleybus photo using one of its standard Leyland Atlanteans with Roe bodywork, to encourage interest in this type of bus.

*Right:* A later West Yorkshire PTE mocked-up trolleybus, this time based on the Optare Delta single-decker.

*Left:* South Yorkshire PTE went one stage further and built a trolleybus based on its standard Dennis Dominator/Alexander R type combination and this was tested on track with overhead erected near Doncaster racecourse. The bus is now at the trolleybus museum at Sandtoft. *J. R. Laming*

*Below:* Southampton Citybus used a fleet of CNG-fuelled Dennis Dart/Plaxton Pointers, dubbed Eco Buses.

*Above:* Claimed as 'the first purpose-built compressed natural gas-powered bus', a Dart/Pointer used by FirstBus in Bristol.

*Right:* Arriva placed LPG-powered DAF SB220/Plaxton Prestige buses in service on Chester park-&-ride services in 1999.

# Bending the Rules

In the UK the way bus operators provided more seats for their passengers was traditionally the use of double-deckers. When single-deckers and double-deckers were roughly the same length you could squeeze 56, maybe 60 into a double-decker against 35/39 in a single-decker. During the 1950s these totals rose to around 78 and 45 as longer buses were legalised, and the totals continued to grow.

Elsewhere in the world with a few notable exceptions like Berlin, Hong Kong and Singapore, the way to cram people on to buses was often to make many of them stand, something UK passengers have proved reluctant to do. And when they needed bigger buses they moved to articulated vehicles that could be as much as 18m long–

nearly twice the length of a British double-decker–accommodating up to 200 passengers, few of them seated.

But while most British operators were buying double-deckers or longer single-deckers there was an undercurrent of interest in artics. South Yorkshire PTE was the first operator to convert that interest into action. The PTE, jointly with Leyland and the Department of Transport, set up a test programme to assess what place artics might

Leyland brought this Leyland-DAB-Saurer across to the UK to capitalise on South Yorkshire's known interest in articulated buses, and the left-hand drive bus is seen on test in Sheffield in July 1977. *D. Muscroft*

MAN built this right-hand drive version of its standard SG192R artic model and coined the term Bendibus, which has stuck with this type.

have in the UK market. In 1977 an 18m DAB artic built by Leyland's Danish subsidiary did a quick tour of Britain and spent three days on trial in passenger-carrying service in Sheffield – special dispensation had to be granted and the bus operated on a no-fares basis.

Then in 1978 a German-built MAN SG192R artic arrived in Britain for service in South Yorkshire; this was the first right-hand drive artic for UK service and paved the way for a proper experiment involving five MANs and five Leylands. The MANs were based on their standard artic model, but the Leylands were a combination of Group resources – a Danish-built DAB chassis and a British-built body incorporating Leyland National parts. A free circular service in Sheffield started in September 1979, but following the 1980 Transport Act the use of artics on fare-paying services was legalised, so in 1981 SYPTE started charging fares – low fares, admittedly, in line with the PTE's fares policy. Later in 1981 staff problems forced the PTE to withdraw the artics. As these had been leased, they lay unused for some time until other operators started to use them.

It looked as if the UK interest in artics had peaked. Certainly there was no sign of enthusiasm among operators, who in all honesty had much greater fish to fry – like the prospect of deregulation and privatisation.

This didn't stop the manufacturers bringing artics across to the UK. Volvo had sent a Stockholm B10M artic to the UK for operators to inspect in 1979 and Mercedes-Benz sent an O.305G rear-engined artic across.

Airlines and airport ground handling operators saw a potential for artics as airside buses, so British Airways bought seven Leyland/DAB artics similar to the SYPTE buses and Luton Airport took three O.305G artics.

There was a glimmer of interest in articulated coaches, and Park's of Hamilton had ordered two Volvo B10M artics with Duple Dominant bodies for its Glasgow-London service before legislation was introduced banning artics from the fast lane of motorways. The order was cancelled.

And so it looked as if the UK's brief flirtation with artics was over. But then South Yorkshire PTE ordered 13 Leyland-DAB artics; ten three-door 61-seaters went into service on the PTE's City Clipper service and three two-door 67-seaters went into service in Rotherham. These were destined to last rather longer in service.

There were other brief flurries of interest. Ulsterbus

bought two Volvo B10M/Van Hool artics for express commuter services in 1993 and another two in 1996. But it took one of the fast-growing new groups that had risen out of the privatisation of NBC, SBG and municipal operators to revive the interest in a big way. Grampian received a Mercedes-Benz O.405G with Alexander 60-seat bodywork in 1992 and following Grampian's merger with Badgerline in 1995 and the creation of FirstBus, First has been an enthusiastic artic user, buying more than 200, a mix of Volvo B10BLA and B7LA, Scania L94UA and Mercedes-Benz Citaro. Stagecoach also bought artics, but stuck to coaches for interurban work for its non-London fleet.

The largest concentration of artics is in London – though for how much longer is not clear, in view of Mayor Boris Johnson's declaration shortly after taking office that the existing fleet would be withdrawn over a number of years.

Artics came to London following a trial with borrowed First artics, and the first of London's large Citaro fleet entered service in 2002. These were operated by Go-Ahead's London fleets and were followed by similar buses for Arriva, First and Stagecoach in London and their multi-door layout and off-bus ticketing proved ideal for absorbing large numbers of passengers arriving at mainline railway stations and getting them to their destinations quickly.

The artic clearly has attractions for some operators. Apart from that first Grampian Merc, all of the newer-generation artics for bus work have been low-floor buses, and artics do offer easier access to more seats than the lower deck of a low-floor double-decker. And with concerns about security in some areas, many passengers favour artics because the driver is always in view, except, perhaps on First ftr vehicles, adapted Volvos with Wright StreetCar bodies designed to look less bus-like and more tram-like. Here the driver is in a compartment at the front and has no direct interaction with passengers, but there are 'customer service hosts' in the main part of the bus to issue tickets.

So, after some false starts, artics are a regular part of the scene in many parts of Britain, though the dislike of artics in London, which appears to have been based on some spurious statistics about accidents involving cyclists, will see their demise there. On some routes they may not be mourned, but on the Red Arrow routes where the artics were the equivalent of Underground trains, mopping up passengers through their doors and speeding them across central London, they proved to be ideal.

South Yorkshire PTE bought both Leyland and MAN artics for its free City Clipper service in Sheffield, and one of each type is seen in 1981. The Leylands used DAB chassis and bodies incorporating Leyland National parts. *T. W. Moore*

*Right:* The first South Yorkshire artics were short-lived in service there. The MANs passed to Midland Red North, and one is seen in 1986. *Adrian Pearson*

*Below:* McGill's of Barrhead used some of the South Yorkshire Leylands on its Glasgow-Barrhead service.

*Above:* One of the second-generation South Yorkshire artics, a Leyland-DAB in Sheffield on the Clipper service. *Kevin Lane*

*Left:* The father of modern artics was this Grampian Mercedes-Benz O.405G of 1992, and Grampian's successor, First, drove the recent interest in artics in the UK.

# No Longer Dominant

For years Duple was *the* name in British coachbuilding. It had been founded in 1919 to build bodies for cars and other light vehicles but in the late 1920s it was becoming recognised as a builder of attractive and well-built coaches and its close links with Bedford chassis brought Duple bodies into a wider range of fleets.

There were competitors, of course, but Duple outlasted most of them, even acquiring a few along the way, notably Burlingham. However, its major competitor emerged as Plaxton, which had been building well-regarded coach bodies in Scarborough since the years after World War I but had really come into its own in the late 1950s and early 1960s with a range of bodies that appealed to a much wider audience. Plaxton's production caught up with Duple's in 1969 just at the time Duple was planning a move from its traditional home in Hendon, North London, to Blackpool, following its 1960 purchase of the Burlingham business. By the time the move to Blackpool was complete, in 1970, Plaxton sales were more than double Duple's.

The Duple Laser looked good and although it sold fairly well, Duple was haemorrhaging market share to Plaxton at the time. This is a Leyland Tiger for Maidstone & District's Invictaway operation.

Duple fought back and had narrowed the gap with Plaxton by 1972 when a new coach range was introduced. The Duple Dominant was an entirely new metal-framed body range, broadly similar in outline to Plaxton's well-regarded Elite range. This helped Duple to keep annual sales levels around the 1,000 mark, although Plaxton sales were typically around 1,400.

Express coach service deregulation in 1980 had a serious impact on Duple. Operators moved away from the lightweight chassis from Bedford and Ford that had represented a substantial proportion of Duple's output and bought increasing numbers of heavyweight coaches, often with bodies from the growing list of European bodybuilders that were selling into the UK market.

*Above:* The Laser's contemporary was the high-floor Caribbean, here on Leyland Tiger for South Wales Transport's contribution to National Express's Rapide services.

*Left:* At the same time Duple got involved in producing the integral Calypso coach based on a Bova underframe; this had the look of a lower-floor Carribbean.

To regain some of its market Duple announced a new range of coach bodies – the normal-height Laser and high-floor Caribbean. These didn't help and Duple sales in 1983 fell to below 400. Duple also introduced an integral coach, the Calypso, using Bova running units.

In 1983 Duple was sold to the Hestair group, which already owned Dennis, and became Hestair Duple. Redesigned Laser and Caribbean bodies appeared in 1984, along with an impressive coach, the Integral 425. The Laser 2 and Caribbean II been in production for barely a season when yet another new coach body range appeared, the 320 and 340 models.

By this time Duple was selling little more than 200 coach bodies a year, but with the privatisation of National Bus Company, a large number of customers disappeared to concentrate on running buses.

Duple's last real chance was the Dennis Dart midibus, for which Duple produced the original Dartline body. This appeared in October 1988 and the following month Hestair announced that it was selling Dennis and Duple to a management buyout team. Under Trinity Holdings, its new owners, things looked good for Duple, but that didn't last. In July 1989 it was announced that Duple's Blackpool operation was closing down and manufacturing rights and jigs for its 300 series and 425 model were being sold to arch-rival Plaxton.

Duple had been losing money for years and its later coach models, notably the Dominant, had proved to be prone to rust. The Blackpool factory that had been producing over 1,000 bodies a year just a decade earlier produced barely 200 in 1989, and a once-proud name was consigned to the dustbin.

Duple had been killed by a number of factors. There was the declining market, the growing number of imported bodies, the move away from lightweight chassis and the increasing problems with body quality. Its one big chance for survival could have been the Dennis Dart, but nobody knew how successful this would be while Duple was changing hands in 1988/89. The company that would go on to build more bodies on Dennis Dart than any other was, of course, Plaxton.

**DUPLE MODEL LAUNCHES 1982-85**

1982 – Laser, Caribbean
1984 – Laser 2, Caribbean II, 425
1985 – 320, 340

The Laser 2 was an unexpectedly quick reworking of the Laser with a new lower front end and fixed side glazing. This travel-stained example is a Leyland Tiger in the Midland Express fleet. *Adrian Pearson*

*Above:* Hot on the heels of the Laser and Caribbean – and Laser 2 and Caribbean II – came the Duple 320 and 340 models, the type designations equating to their overall height expressed in centimetres. This is a 340 on DAF SB2300 for Peter Carol.

*Below:* The Duple 425 integral was widely regarded as a good coach that never really had a chance against the background of the coachbuilder's troubles and shrinking market share.

# Whatever Happened To...

If in the late 1980s and the 1990s you were asked to put your money on which of the new groupings that were emerging from the privatisation of the National Bus Company would survive, would you, for instance, have identified AJS as a rising star? Or ATL? Or indeed GRT Bus Group? You might have identified Stagecoach as a company with potential; it quickly showed itself to be quite aggressive and seemed to understand the new rules that applied to local bus operations. You might have thought that the sheer size of Badgerline in 1994 guaranteed a bright future. The same could be said of Drawlane. But these are names that are no longer familiar to us, so what happened?

For a start, the bus industry had been regulated for more than half a century, so there wasn't really anybody about with first-hand experience of real competition. And because the deregulation of bus services was taking place at the same time as privatisation of National Bus Company there were many people in the industry who saw this as a once-in-a-lifetime opportunity to run their own bus companies and make serious money into the bargain. Many managers resented what they saw as the dead hand of NBC centralism and wanted to prove what they could do when there were no restrictions.

One problem, of course, was money. If they were to buy their own bus company they needed a friendly bank manager and often they had to re-mortgage their homes. But groups of managers pooled resources and many were successful in the great NBC sell-off. But that was only the start.

After the champagne corks had been popped and the initial euphoria there was the difficult job of running your own bus company without the security of that umbilical cord to NBC headquarters. At least bus companies generate money up front and so cash flow is not always a problem. The problems arose if the new management team found themselves defending their territory from a competitor, or when they had to consider buying new buses. NBC's vehicle replacement programme had slowed in its final years, but what these newly independent operators were often looking for was cheap, almost disposable, minibuses. These tided them over, but the harsh realities of bus operation quickly sunk in and it

seemed like the way to make your money was to sell out and there were plenty of interested buyers.

Within five years of the final NBC sale, the picture was very different. In the NBC sale of 72 major subsidiaries, nearly half had gone initially to management teams. History shows that management teams stood a better chance at the beginning of the sell-off process; most of the first 15 sales went to managers or staff, while only six of the last 15 did. What had happened in the meantime was that management teams that had been successful in the early days were now bidding for and sometimes winning control of companies that were later in the queue. And there was a new type of bidder that recognised the value of bus company ownership but had no previous connection with NBC. Stagecoach is the most obvious example, buying three NBC companies in the sell-off and later mopping up companies whose managers decided to sell on.

Some of the companies that had been successful in the early sell-off felt bold enough to bid for their former sister companies, sometimes with success. Midland Red West bought Bristol Omnibus, Caldaire (West Riding) bought United Auto, Western Travel (Cheltenham & Gloucester) bought Midland Red South, Yorkshire Traction bought Lincolnshire Road Car, and Proudmutual (Northumbria) bought Kentish Bus.

In 1993, five years after the last NBC sell-off the picture was very different. Stagecoach had mopped up a few management buyouts, including significant companies like Ribble and Southdown, and Badgerline had started its expansion with acquisitions like Midland Red West, Eastern National and South Wales Transport.

A new name in 1993 was British Bus, previously known as Drawlane, itself a subsidiary of Endless Holdings. British Bus continued to grow its empire until 1996 when, to the surprise of the industry, it was taken over by the Cowie Group. In bus terms Cowie owned three companies in London – Grey-Green, Leaside and South London, with around 1,000 buses between them. British Bus had over 5,000 buses. But Cowie also had substantial car dealerships as well as the Hughes DAF bus and coach dealership. But while the Drawlane, British Bus and even Cowie names were not readily known to passengers as their bus companies continued to trade under existing names and in existing liveries, that all changed in 1997 when Cowie Group changed its name to Arriva and adopted the now-familiar aquamarine and Cotswold stone corporate livery.

GRT Bus Group, mentioned earlier, grew out of the privatisation of the municipally owned Grampian Transport and had expanded with the purchase of Midland Scottish in the Scottish Bus Group sell-off, as well as Eastern Counties from its management team and the Leicester and Northampton municipal companies. In terms of size GRT was still seen as a relatively small player until it merged in 1995 with Badgerline to create FirstBus. Badgerline with some 4,000 buses was seen as the larger partner to GRT's 1,600 buses. Yet the GRT influence would spread as it became clear that GRT's Aberdeen headquarters would be the centre of power, and of course First has gone on to become a major bus and train operator in Britain with substantial interests in the United States.

The other groups mentioned in the first paragraph didn't fare quite so well.

ATL Holdings, formed by Tony Lavin and the parent company of Carlton PSV (Sales) Ltd, bought National Travel (East) in the early part of the NBC sell-off and the English bit of Crosville towards the end. Within a year ATL had sold Crosville to Drawlane, which left it with some local bus

operations in Leeds and Sheffield and the Carlton dealership. In July 1989, following problems with vehicle maintenance, the remaining parts of the business were sold to National Express, itself a management buyout from NBC.

AJS Holdings was named after its founder, Alan Stephenson who had first indicated his ambition by leading the management buyout of the East Yorkshire company from NBC. This was followed by West Yorkshire Road Car and London Country North East. The group's policy was to establish smaller operating units and in 1989 it split up LCNE, creating County Bus & Coach and Sovereign Bus & Coach, and the West Yorkshire company was subdivided to create Harrogate & District, Keighley & District and York City & District, with the rump being sold on to Yorkshire Rider.

In 1990 AJS was buying up smaller operators to strengthen its Home Counties operations but then sold the bulk of its Stevenage operation to Luton & District. Then York City & District was sold to Yorkshire Rider, although

The first new double-deckers bought by Western Travel were Alexander RL-bodied Leyland Olympians in 1990 like this one in the Swindon & District fleet. When Western Travel sold out to Stagecoach these buses – virtually Stagecoach standards – fitted well with their new owners. *D. A. Russell/D. M. Pemberton*

a new AJS subsidiary, Yorkshire Coastliner, retained some of the York fleet. Back in the south, a controlling interest in the County business was sold to its chairman.

Then in 1991 Blazefield Holdings, formed by two AJS directors, acquired a 75 per cent share in the seven remaining AJS operating companies – essentially the Yorkshire and Sovereign operations, and Blazefield would continue to develop these businesses until 2006 when the group was sold to the expanding French group, Transdev.

There are other groups that blossomed briefly then decided to pull out of bus operation: Q Drive, which was active to the west of London; Transit Holdings, which grew out of Harry Blundred's Devon General buyout; Caldaire Holdings, once a significant name in Yorkshire and north-east England; Proudmutual, with interests in the north and south of England; Western Travel in and around Gloucestershire; and Cawlett in the south-west of England.

Yet all were gone within a few years, mostly selling out to the bigger groups that history told us would probably emerge from the late 1980s and early 1990s sell-offs anyway. Some disappeared because it all proved to be too much and the initial optimism turned sour when the realities of bus operation and the need to provide properly maintained buses became clear. Others simply saw an opportunity to make money and went knocking on doors at Aberdeen, Perth or Sunderland, or wherever the head offices of the bigger groups were at the time.

At the time of writing only two of the 72 major NBC subsidiaries are still in independent hands – East Yorkshire and Trent – while most of the others are now controlled by Arriva, First or Stagecoach, following the great carve-up that gave us the company structure we know today.

The buyout teams may have failed because they didn't achieve their dream of running their own bus companies and perhaps growing to become one of the major players, but few of them emerged without a bit of money in the bank, and the really good managers were recognised by the increasingly dominant mega-groups and offered jobs.

Q Drive's Bee Line operation operated to the west of London. This Leyland Olympian/Northern Counties is seen in 1989 in Reading. *C. D. Jones*

# National Service

The much-reviled Leyland National was not a bad bus – well, eventually it was OK – but it was probably not the bus that its main customer really needed.

It was born in the late 1960s when the UK bus-operating and bus-manufacturing sectors were going through major changes. Leyland had mopped up most of the competition to create the giant British Leyland Motor Corporation, building cars, trucks and buses. The buses were the models inherited from AEC, Bristol, Daimler and Guy, plus Leyland's own range. On the operating side the state-owned Transport Holding Company and the private BET Group merged to form the National Bus Company.

The two new giants, British Leyland and National Bus, quickly announced a joint venture, Leyland National Company, to build a new single-deck bus in a new plant near Workington, on the Cumbrian coast.

On paper, the joint venture made sense. NBC had a fleet of some 20,000 buses, the majority built by companies now under BLMC, but these were a fairly mixed bunch. Transport Holding Company had pursued a very standardised vehicle policy, buying mainly from its in-house chassis and body plants, Bristol and Eastern Coach Works. BET had a less standardised approach and company managers had greater freedom to specify the buses they required.

Some degree of standardisation clearly made economic sense, but it is fair to say that the product of the joint venture, the Leyland National, was not necessarily what NBC managers might be wanting.

The National was a bold departure from everything that had gone before. Buses were still largely hand-built and Leyland had identified the need for buses to be built on the

Although the Leyland National was extensively tested in prototype form, it proved to be less durable in the heavy hands of bus drivers and mechanics.

type of production lines it saw at the car factories it acquired. The ideas led to a concept bus, the Commutabus, a single-deck integrally constructed bus with a one-step entrance leading to a bright and spacious flat floor saloon. The Commutabus was shelved, but many of its features were resurrected in the new Leyland National.

Single-deck buses were enjoying a resurgence in the 1960s, with many significant operators turning away from double-deckers because at the time only single-deckers were permitted to be used on a driver-only basis. Many city fleets that had previously only included token numbers of single-deckers, usually to cope with low bridges or low-demand routes, started buying the new breed of rear-engined single-deckers that began to appear in the early 1960s. For interurban operators, there was also the opportunity to replace life-expired lowbridge double-deckers with 53 or 55

seats with driver-only single-deckers that offered the same capacity, plus a greater number of standing passengers.

Against this background the National was born, though the government had thrown a couple of spanners in the works. Firstly, in 1966 driver-only *double*-deckers had been legalised, and some – though by no means all – of the operators that had switched to single-deckers chose to switch back. And then there was the New Bus Grants scheme, introduced in 1968 to encourage bus companies to update their fleets with new buses suitable for driver-only operation. This offered them up to 25 per cent of the cost of a new bus; this rose to 50 per cent before the scheme was phased out in the 1980s.

Bus operators, never slow to grab a bargain, went on a buying spree, and while the Bus Grants scheme certainly helped the Leyland National, it also worked against it because

*Right and below:* The Super National Business Commuter was one attempt to broaden the model's appeal. The interior view suggests it was an interesting concept, but there were no takers.

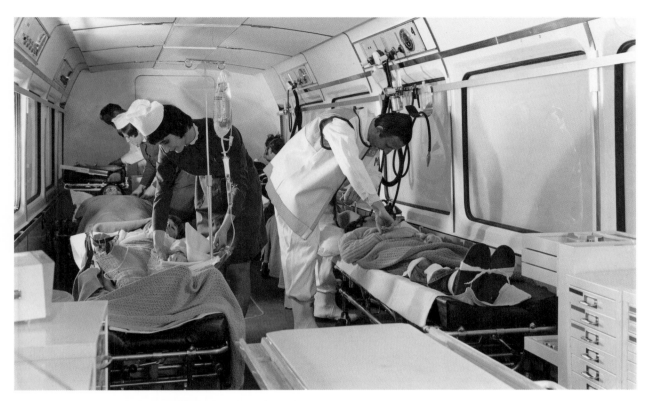

*Above and left:* The Leyland Lifeliner was another concept bus, a fully-equipped casualty unit, but it never caught on.

many operators built up fleets of new double-deckers, notably the Passenger Transport Executives that had been set up around the same time in major conurbations.

The National was unveiled to the world at the 1970 Commercial Motor Show and was shown to be quite unlike anything that had been seen before. The body carried forward no design touches from previous Leyland group products and was designed with the maximum number of standard panels in two basic lengths, 10.3m and 11.3m. The most unusual design feature was the pod mounted at the rear of the roof, housing the heating and ventilating equipment.

Underneath the National had a turbocharged Leyland 510 fixed-head engine, a new unit based on the 500 series developed for trucks. Air suspension was standard and

Leyland did have some success with National-based railcars and diesel units. This is a prototype.

low-profile tyres helped to keep the floor level down. The production line at Workington was designed to produce 2,000 Nationals a year, with a small workforce.

National Bus had to keep its part of the bargain and ordered 498 pretty well off the drawing board. These were for a range of former THC and NBC companies, and this order was quickly followed by another from NBC, for 520 more. With orders from other UK fleets, it looked as if the National was off to a good start.

To help the National on its way, British Leyland fairly quickly deleted other models from its lists, like the AEC Swift, Bristol RE, Daimler Roadliner and Fleetline single-deck and Leyland Panther – in fact any rear-engined bus model from its range that might divert customers away from the National. While some of these types may have gone unmourned, there was concern that the Bristol RE was on the way out. It had been the first rear-engined single-deck bus chassis, in 1962, and had been shown to be by far the best. While British customers were denied the RE, Ulsterbus in Northern Ireland was not enamoured of the National and made it clear that it would shop elsewhere if it couldn't buy REs. As an 'export' customer, Ulsterbus continued to receive REs well into the 1980s.

For a new concept the production line worked very well and supported Leyland's belief that buses could be produced in the same way as cars. But the bus itself was proving to be

a problem. The 510 engine was new to the National's customers and engineers are often suspicious of units they don't know. For companies used to chunky Gardner 6LX or Leyland 680 engines, the 510 was a different animal altogether. Worse still, it turned out to be unreliable and prone to be smoky, and the National quickly gained an unenviable reputation, but with National Bus on board and placing repeat orders its sales figures continued to look healthy – even though the Workington plant would never reach its 2,000-a-year potential.

Leyland fiddled with the specification – there was the 1978-introduced B-series, a cheaper and simpler version – but eventually gave in to pressure from operators to make the National a more acceptable bus. But not before Leyland tried to broaden the National's appeal by producing a range of variations on the National theme. There was the Business Commuter, a high-tech vehicle for business people; the Suburban Express, with a raised floor at the front to give a flat gangway; the Lifeliner, a mobile casualty and communications centre for emergency use; Mobile Branches for the Midland Bank; and even halfcab airside buses for British Airways. There were even railbuses and diesel units for British Rail that were rather obviously based on the National. And if you think some of this smacks of desperation to keep the production lines fed, then you could be right.

Leyland's solution to the National's problems was a significant makeover that saw the radiator moved to the front, resulting in a more bulbous appearance, and 'proper' engines, derivatives of the popular Leyland 680 unit, the L11 and turbocharged TL11. These gave the new National 2 model a boost and attracted new customers who may have been suspicious of the 510 engine, and Leyland even quietly introduced a Gardner engine option in 1983 after operators had shown that a Gardner could be shoe-horned into the engine bay.

The last Nationals were built in 1985, and in 14 years of production some 7,700 were built – an impressive total until you recall that Workington could have turned out more than three times that number if working at total capacity, something it never did.

The National enjoyed an Indian summer in the deregulated post-1986 world when it proved to be a useful competitive tool for large and small operators alike. By this time many had been re-engined with Cummins, DAF or Volvo engines, but the body structure – long regarded as literally its strongest selling-point – proved virtually indestructible. East Lancs even rebuilt 176 Nationals as Greenways, lengthening their lives substantially.

If you sell more than 7,700 examples of any type of bus it can hardly be regarded as a blunder, yet it was patently not the bus that was required at the time, and despite Leyland's well-publicised testing on Belgian pavé, in the heat of Spain and the cold of northern Finland, it was only when it was placed in the hands of bus drivers and mechanics that its shortcomings became clearer.

### LEYLAND NATIONAL TIMELINE

| | |
|---|---|
| 1969 | British Leyland and National Bus Company form Leyland National Company |
| 1970 | Launched at Earls Court show |
| 1972 | Prototype handed over to Cumberland Motor Services |
| 1978 | Simpler B-series announced |
| 1978 | Phase II version announced |
| 1978 | Prototype National 2 shown |
| 1979 | Production Leyland National 2 shown |
| 1980 | First production National 2 delivered |
| 1985 | Last National 2 delivered (to Halton) |

*Left:* Some operators decided they could improve on the National. Eastern Counties fitted a front radiator and a Gardner 6HLX engine to this bus. *M. Fowler*

*Left:* The Leyland National Greenway was a more radical reworking of the bus by East Lancs. This is the prototype.

# Stick With What You Know

Traditionally, the demand for new coaches peaked just after Easter. Coach operators wanted to parade new hardware for their clients (and at coach rallies for their competitors) to see at the start of each summer season, to prove that they still ran a business successful enough to allow them to continue to invest.

That left a hole for coachbuilders; with expensive factories and year-round staff, they needed to keep the accountants happy and while there was sometimes an acceptance that staff might go off to run bed & breakfast establishments or sell ice-cream during the peak season, it made sense to keep the factory ticking over.

It is perhaps no surprise that the big names in British coachbuilding were based at the seaside where this seasonality could be managed: Harrington at Hove, Plaxton at Scarborough, and Duple, initially in north London but ultimately in Blackpool following the acquisition of Burlingham.

One way to keep your factory going was to build service buses, where seasonality was less important. While the

The Weymann Fanfare was more successful than most coach bodies produced by bus bodybuilders. This is a 1958 AEC Reliance/Fanfare for Neath & Cardiff.

# MCW Fanfare

## *for maximum comfort over any distance*

North Western

★ All-steel framework of great strength.

★ Spacious interior of modern design with wide, well-padded luggage rack.

★ Luxury seating for 37-41 passengers.

★ Designed for easy convertibility from coach to bus.

★ Maximum comfort for the driver.

✳ *Please write for full particulars of this outstanding coach.*

**METROPOLITAN · CAMMELL · WEYMANN LIMITED**
VICKERS HOUSE, WESTMINSTER, LONDON S.W.1

A 1955 MCW advert for the Fanfare coach features a North Western AEC Reliance, with 'all-steel framework of great strength' as a selling point in the days of wooden-framed mainstream coaches.

coachbuilders achieved some success with the big bus companies, more often they sold to smaller independent operators who already bought their coaches.

But when it was the other way round and bus bodybuilders turned their hand to coaches, it didn't really work. For a start, buses are needed all year round so there is no off-season. And although some attractive coaches were produced, they often didn't appeal to smaller companies that had no real relationship with them.

They all tried it.

Take MCW. Up there with the biggest bus bodybuilders, churning out bus bodies by the yard at the Metro-Cammell factory at Elmdon and in smaller quantities at the Weymann factory at Addlestone. It had dabbled quite

successfully in the coach market – selling mainly to BET Group companies who were already buying its bus bodies – with the Weymann Fanfare in 1954, building 144. The Fanfare was not unattractive, and when 36ft-long vehicles were legalised, a longer version – the Castilian – was built for Southdown.

For reasons that are difficult to understand, in 1962 MCW decided to have a go at building coach bodies on lighter-weight Bedford chassis. At the time there were many small operators buying Bedford coaches, usually with Burlingham, Duple or Plaxton bodies – bodies that were often of composite construction: that is, wooden framed with metal reinforcement, which made it easier for smaller operators to repair them. Bus bodies, on the other

*Above:* The MCW Topaz was one of the less attractive bodies on Bedford's twin-steer VAL chassis. This is the 1962 prototype – in fact, the only one built. Note the bus-like straight waist and the heavily hooded front windscreen.

*Right:* Inside this 1965 MCW brochure for the Topaz II it claims that the body 'has Classic Lines, 20th Century Comfort and a Great Future'. It could be said that MCW was wrong on all three counts – although the coach looked better than the fairly dreadful artist's impression.

MCW **TOPAZ** II

The MCW Amethyst was an equally uninspired 41-seat coach body on Bedford SB chassis.

hand, were typically metal-framed, using aluminium or steel. Metro-Cammell had only ever built metal-framed bodies, so its new coach design was metal-framed too.

The MCW Topaz body was mounted on Bedford's new twin-steer VAL chassis, but only one was built. The Topaz resurfaced as the 52-seat Topaz II in 1965, again on VAL; six were built. At the same time MCW launched the 41-seat Amethyst on Bedford SB chassis; one was built. In 1966 a new coach body was introduced, the Athena, on Bedford VAM, and it reappeared with attractive restyling as the Metropolitan, 33 of which were built between 1967 and 1969. In 1969 the coach bodywork was contracted to Strachans, who built 10 Metropolitans on Ford R192 chassis.

What MCW discovered – as did other bus builders dipping a toe in the coach market – was that the Duples and Plaxtons of this world had a proven track record, had established dealer networks and their products retained their value; important when these were being traded in against new coaches. The bus market didn't work that way.

Park Royal also had a couple of stabs at the coach market. In 1954 it produced some fairly straightforward metal-framed coaches for Neath & Cardiff and Bourne & Balmer, and later in the year launched the Royalist, a centre-entrance coach that had more than a passing resemblance to the contemporary ECW coach body that was becoming familiar in state-owned fleets. This was no coincidence as Bill Shirley, Park Royal's recently appointed director and general manager, came from ECW. The Royalist didn't set the heather on fire.

Nor did the next Royalist, 12 years later. This was an attempt by British Leyland to break into the lightweight coach market and it was a not unattractive coach – wood-framed, surprisingly, when Park Royal otherwise built metal-framed bodies. This may have been a move to attract smaller operators, but instead of offering the new Royalist on Bedford or Ford chassis, it used an in-house chassis: the rear-engined Albion Viking VK43AL. This chassis, favoured by Scottish Bus Group for lighter duties, was not familiar to small operators and only five were built.

Another bodybuilder in the British Leyland fold was Roe, which back in the 1950s (when it had been part of the ACV Group) produced a series of attractive Duple-like coaches carrying the Dalesman name. The first was introduced in 1954, and updated versions appeared in 1955, 1956 and 1959, though the last were built in 1960. A total of 68 were built, with Essex County Coaches the main customer. Most were built on AEC Reliance chassis, also supplied from inside the ACV Group.

AMETHYST by
METROPOLITAN·CAMMELL·WEYMANN LIMITED
41 SEAT SINGLE DECK COACH BODY

Roe found itself producing luxury coaches more than 20 years later, perhaps reluctantly as part of Leyland Bus. The coach was the Leyland Royal Tiger Doyen, a high-quality rear-engined semi-integral coach that would, in theory, do battle with the likes of MAN, Neoplan and Setra who were sniffing around the UK market. Most coaches for UK operators were still mid-engined, but Leyland decided that a rear-engined model was needed.

Launched in 1982, it was certainly an attractive coach and Leyland decided that the underframe and body would be built by Roe at Leeds, still a fairly traditional bus bodybuilder. Things didn't go well: deliveries slipped, and main production was switched to Leyland's Workington plant, with Roe left to concentrate on high-specification models. The model was also available as an underframe, the Royal Tiger, for bodying by other builders, in practice only Plaxton and Van Hool.

The Royal Tiger and Doyen continued in production until 1988 in spite of poor sales, but it was not sales that killed the model. In 1988 Volvo Bus acquired Leyland Bus and the Doyen was an early casualty. Barely 100 complete Doyens and 64 underframes were built during the model's six years in production.

Undaunted by its earlier lack of success, MCW launched itself back into coaches, recognising – as Leyland had done – that express service deregulation would boost the need

MCW bounced back in 1966 with the Athena coach, on Bedford VAM chassis. This would be the only one built.

for new coaches, often among customers already familiar with MCW's bus products.

First was the Metroliner double-decker, a 4.2m-long three-axle coach based on chassis that had previously been supplied to Hong Kong operators. National Bus Company and Scottish Bus Group companies were the first and, it would turn out, the main customers. NBC took over 100 of the 123 built, but it proved to be a troublesome vehicle. Three 4m-high 400GT integral models were built in 1987/88, but these would be the last Metroliners as MCW was now concentrating on producing its successful Metrobus and Metrorider types.

A single-deck Metroliner followed in 1983 and 42 were built in two versions until 1987. Again NBC and SBG companies were the best customers.

It is fair to say that other bus builders fared rather better when they turned to coaches, often at the request of existing bus customers who they couldn't afford to disappoint. Alexander's legendary Y type body started as a coach and proved to be an adaptable design that looked equally at home with smaller side windows as a bus and panoramic windows as a coach – though more typically, Y type coaches were strictly dual-purpose vehicles that could double on long-distance express and shorter interurban bus journeys. The same was true of the Y type's successor, the T type. Alexander's most dramatic coach design was the 12m-long M type, built from

1968 on Bristol REMH and Leyland Leopard chassis, which was designed for long overnight journeys and included features that would soon become more widespread, including smaller side windows and double-glazing.

When Alexander facelifted the T type body the range broadened into TC luxury coaches, TE express coaches, and TS service buses. With direct glazing, the TC was an attractive coach but SBG fleets were its main customers.

Willowbrook too achieved some success in the coach market – though like Alexander it was typically selling these to larger customers – with the 008 Spacecar of 1974 and the simpler 003 of 1979 that was built in reasonable quantities for NBC fleets.

ECW enjoyed success with its simple but attractive coach bodies for Bristol LS and MW, but its return to the coach market in 1982, under Leyland Bus, was less happy. Its unnamed body, coded B51 by Leyland, was a straightforward design that was built on Leyland Leopard and Tiger chassis for NBC and Selnec, but it suffered from structural problems that resulted in many being rebodied.

On the other hand, firms like Duple and Plaxton, whose main business was based on luxury coach bodies, produced some decent and well-regarded bus bodies over the years, more recently with the Duple Dominant Bus and 300, and the Plaxton Derwent and Bustler. Plaxton of course, ironically, went on to become a major supplier to the bus market when its Pointer body, developed for the Dennis Dart chassis by its subsidiary, Reeve Burgess, became what was probably the most successful post-war British bus body.

*Above:* The Athena resurfaced early in 1967 with an attractive facelift as the Metropolitan, which enjoyed some success. This could be the 1966 Athena prototype rebuilt.

*Below:* Park Royal's first Royalist body was very similar to contemporary ECW coach designs, though with a curved waistrail and centre entrance. This is a 1955 Birch AEC Reliance.

*Above right:* In this contemporary advert, MCW pitches its Metropolitan against the Duples and Plaxtons that most operators went for if they needed a lightweight coach – and in spite of the MCW offer (which even included a mud flap) they continued to support Duple and Plaxton.

*Above:* The next Park Royal Royalist was a Leyland product, mounted on Albion Viking VK43L rear-engined chassis. The ribbed side panels will be noted – possibly not its most practical feature.

*Right:* A 1968 Albion advert features the Park Royal Royalist coach offering 'VIP comfort', 'easy high performance' and 'highly stable, effortless and predictable handling'. In truth, the rather agricultural Viking VK43 chassis was hardly the most sophisticated base for what was a not unattractive-looking coach.

# 32 ft...
# and smooth with it

If you want a coach chassis that's long on luxury and short on costs, look no further than the rear-engined Viking. For VIP passenger comfort with the Viking's 54 in. front and 64 in. rear semi-elliptic springs. For ample luggage accommodation— spacious lockers fit within the wheelbase. For easy high performance—the 125 bhp Leyland O.400 diesel combines with an almost constant 30/70 front-to-rear distribution of the Viking's low weight . . . ensures highly stable, effortless and predictable handling under all conditions. And for a worthwhile bonus in tyre economy—loadings on each tyre are virtually equal.
Consider your passengers, consider a Viking: Gross laden weight as a coach: 9½ ton.

## VIKING VK43AL
### REAR-ENGINED COACH CHASSIS

ALBION MOTORS LTD. SCOTSTOUN, GLASGOW. W4. Tel: Scotstoun 1261-70
Overseas Sales: Berkeley Square House, Berkeley Square, London, W1. Tel: 01-499 6050

*Above:* A 1957 Roe Dalesman coach on Leyland Tiger Cub chassis for Teesside Railless Traction Board. The Dalesman range, owing something to Duple designs, were attractive vehicles.

*Left:* Much later Roe was chosen to build Leyland's integral Royal Tiger Doyen coach, an attempt to match the best European integrals. This Doyen was built for Merthyr Tydfil Transport.

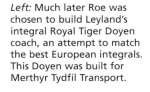

*Left:* MCW returned to coaches with its Metroliner models. This single-decker has the original, rather flat front end with a slightly asymmetric front screen. This East Kent example is liveried for National Holidays work.

Above: The Metroliner was reworked as a rather impressive high-floor coach. *T. W. Moore*

*Right:* The 1975 Willowbrook Spacecar was an impressive coach body from a smaller bus builder. *T. W. Moore*

*Above:* East Lancs produced a rather startling coach body in 1974/75, mounted on Seddon RU (one for Hyndburn) and Leyland Leopard chassis (two for Halton). This is a 1975 Halton Leopard leaving London's Victoria Coach Station on hire to Crosville in 1976. *C. Nash*

*Below:* Alexander reworked its ugly duckling T type dual-purpose body as a not unattractive coach, the TC type. This is the prototype on Leyland Tiger chassis for Scottish Citylink express coach duties.

*Right:* When the tables were turned and builders of luxury coaches turned to buses, the result was usually more successful. This is Plaxton's Bustler, built between 1980 and 1986 and the side elevation is clearly based on the contemporary Plaxton Supreme coach body. This demonstrator is on Bedford YMT chassis.

*Below:* Duple also turned out some attractive buses, like the Dominant Bus, here on a short 1976 Leyland Leopard for Chester.

# Little Things Mean a Lot

It always seemed so blatantly obvious. Bus services that were lightly loaded didn't need big buses; a small bus would solve all the problems. Well, yes, but drivers still had to be paid big-bus rates, the unions saw to that, so any savings that could be made on the cost of buying and running a small bus were pretty well cancelled out by the cost of wages.

That didn't stop bus manufacturers from developing smaller buses, and while some never actually reached production and others were built only in limited quantities, it wasn't necessarily because they were bad buses, but because they were the right buses at the wrong time. Then when the time *was* right, it took manufacturers some time to produce anything that was much more than a panel van with seats.

For the first 40 years or so after World War II, it was all about capacity. Operators clamoured to squeeze as many seats as possible into their buses and manufacturers did what they could to help. Single-deckers were first a maximum of 27ft 6in long (39/40 seats), then 30ft long (44/45 seats), then 36ft long (53/55 seats); double-deckers were first 26ft long (56/58 seats), then 30ft long (73/74 seats), then rear-engined (77/78 seats).

There was no room for smaller buses, it seemed. When operators that really needed smaller buses placed orders, it was for adapted goods chassis, in the case of David MacBrayne, or small coach chassis like the Bedford VAS. These could be used for driver-only operation, but a bus with its entrance ahead of the front wheels was clearly preferable.

Albion tried with the little mid-engined Nimbus which remained in production between 1955 and 1963; London Transport created the Guy Special GS type for its Country operations; Dennis produced small normal control buses for Aldershot & District and East Kent; Bristol and ECW built the front-engined SC and the mid-engined SU for Tilling fleets.

The Albion Nimbus was Leyland's 1950s attempt to build a smaller bus. This former Halifax 1963 Nimbus NS3AN/Weymann is seen after sale to Wiles, Port Seton. *Gavin Booth*

*Above:* Not all Albion Nimbus chassis carried such attractive bodywork. This 1960 Nimbus NS3N for Guernsey Railway Company had a rather anachronistic body by Reading of Portsmouth.

*Right:* Although sales were disappointing, Albion continued to improve and promote the Nimbus. This 1958 advert introduces the NS3AL version and features a Devon General Willowbrook-bodied example.

But while these models were built to suit particular needs, usually lightly loaded rural routes that could be operated without a conductor, the idea of using small buses in an urban environment was never really considered. In the towns and cities – and between them – big buses were best.

There was change in the air at the start of the 1970s, however. Seddon, not exactly a big name in buses, produced a neat little 25-seat front-engined/front-entrance bus with its own bodywork and christened it the Pennine 4.236 Midi. It was a name waiting to be used – well, the Midi bit anyway. BMC had introduced the Mini car in 1959 and the Maxi in 1969, so the word midi became the generic description for buses that were neither van-based minibuses or purpose-built big buses. Looking back, the name was more successful than Seddon's little bus, but a few operators chose them for innovative urban services, notably Selnec PTE and Edinburgh Corporation.

Alexander had a go with its S type midibus, a 27-seater based on Ford A series running units, and although it was a neat little bus, and sold to NBC, SBG and PTE fleets, the A series did not turn out to be Ford's finest hour.

Then in 1978 Bedford dusted off a design that had been produced by the bodybuilder Marshall, sent it to the General

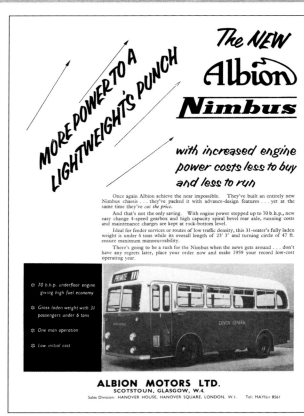

The **NEW**
Albion
**Nimbus**

*MORE POWER TO A LIGHTWEIGHT'S PUNCH*

*with increased engine power costs less to buy and less to run*

Once again Albion achieve the near impossible. They've built an entirely new Nimbus chassis . . . they've packed it with advance-design features . . . yet at the same time they've *cut the price.*

And that's not the only saving. With engine power stepped up to 70 b.h.p., new easy change 4-speed gearbox and high capacity spiral bevel rear axle, running costs and maintenance charges are kept at rock-bottom level.

Ideal for feeder services or routes of low traffic density, this 31-seater's fully laden weight is under 6 tons while its overall length of 23′ 3″ and turning circle of 47 ft. ensure maximum manoeuvrability.

There's going to be a rush for the Nimbus when the news gets around . . . don't have any regrets later, place your order now and make 1959 your record low-cost operating year.

✧ 70 b.h.p. underfloor engine giving high fuel economy

✧ Gross laden weight with 31 passengers under 6 tons

✧ One man operation

✧ Low initial cost

**ALBION MOTORS LTD.**
SCOTSTOUN, GLASGOW, W.4.
Sales Division: HANOVER HOUSE, HANOVER SQUARE, LONDON, W.1.   Tel: MAYfair 8561

Motors design studio and ended up with a singularly attractive rear-engined 27-seat minibus. Only four were built before the GM plug was pulled, which many felt was a great pity. A design, perhaps, that was ahead of its time.

That time was just around the corner, though nobody knew it. The combined effect of the deregulation of local bus services in 1986 and the parallel privatisation of National Bus Company created a market for small urban buses. There had been minibus experiments before this, often using Ford Transits, but it took Harry Blundred, managing director of the Devon General company, to prove to the world that high-frequency 16-seat minibuses driven by new drivers paid at a lower rate than 'big bus' drivers, could attract custom, particularly where the previous choice was a lumbering great Bristol VRT every half hour.

The economic climate in the mid-1980s did not encourage investment in expensive new buses, particularly by former NBC companies that were now run by their managers whose houses and savings were on the line. The minibus was the weapon chosen by many of the new entrants to the newly competitive bus market, and the incumbent operators had to fight fire with fire.

As operators clamoured for small buses the Ford Transit, Freight Rover Sherpa and Iveco Daily were the main choices in the 16-20-seat range, with the Dodge 50 (later badged as Renault) and Mercedes-Benz L608 picking up

In 1970 Leeds City Transport
bought Mercedes-Benz
406Ds converted by
Deansgate for a shoppers'
service in the city centre.
These were predecessors
of the thousands of
'breadvans' that would
flood Britain's roads in the
mid-1980s.

sales in the next size range. These small buses made economic sense – you sent along to the local garage for spares, for instance – but were not much fun for passengers who were crammed into a restricted body that had originally been designed as a parcel van.

The so-called breadvans helped many businesses to ride out the initial excesses of competition, but soon operators were finding that 16-seaters were too small, and looked for something larger and more customer-friendly.

This prompted two new arrivals on the scene in 1986. MCW designed a purpose-built front-engined minibus, the 25-seat Metrorider, and went on to enjoy some success with this. Optare, a new arrival on the scene following Leyland's closure of the Roe body plant at Leeds, designed a stylish 25-seat minibus around the Volkswagen LT55 and called it the CityPacer.

This opened the eyes of operators who realised that small buses needn't be a compromise and that passengers deserved something better than breadvans, and something that actually *looked* good as well. Optare bought the rights to the

Metrorider on the closure of MCW's bus business in 1988, ironed out some of the problems and enjoyed great success with the model, now subtly renamed MetroRider.

And then of course Dennis came along and rewrote the book with the Dart, which could be everything from a midibus to virtually a full-size single-decker. Dennis had produced an earlier midibus, the Domino, which was essentially a scaled-down version of the Dominator double-deck chassis, and therefore probably over-engineered and heavy for the type of work it was called on to do. Only 34 were built, for Greater Manchester and South Yorkshire.

The Nimbus, Midi and JJL failed not because they were bad buses, but because they came along too soon when bus operators didn't think they needed small buses. Then when they did, all they could buy were Transits, Sherpas and the like – none of them bad vehicles in themselves (well, maybe the Sherpa wasn't that good), but hardly the best vehicles to attract passengers with.

Marshall, who had originally come up with the concept bus that became the Bedford JJL, came up with the Marshall Minibus in 1995, a low-floor 8.5m-long rear-engined bus with seats for up to 30 passengers. Where the JJL was a decade too early, the Minibus came along at the right time. The trouble was, it was not a very good bus, and the few customers who bought them new quickly sold them on.

Another attempt to deal with the problem of providing buses in deeply rural areas was the community bus, a Ford Transit driven by local volunteers, a joint venture by National Bus Company and Norfolk County Council.

*Above:* The Seddon Pennine 4 Midi was an attempt to build smaller buses for urban operation and Selnec PTE was a major customer.

*Below:* The chassis of the Seddon Pennine 4.236 Midi was simplicity itself, with the Perkins engine nestling to the driver's left.

The Alexander S type minibus was based on Ford A series units, which proved to be its Achilles' heel. This is a Grampian example.

The Bedford JJL had great potential, but was killed off by General Motors. The rear elevation shows a bus that would still look good 30 years on.

The things politicians are expected to do! Then transport minister, David Mitchell MP flags off the first Hampshire MiniBus services in 1986.

*Above:* A scene that was repeated throughout Britain in the late 1980s – Dormobile-bodied Ford Transits running on the Eastern Counties City Line operation. *G. B. Wise*

*Left:* The Freight Rover Sherpa was the Transit's closest rival, but never proved to be as successful. This is an East Kent Sherpa with 16-seat Dormobile body.

*Right:* The Dennis Domino was an attempt to build a more substantial small urban bus. While it was maybe too substantial – this is a South Yorkshire PTE Optare-bodied Domino – it paved the way for the Dennis Dart, one of the most successful bus types of all time. *Mike Greenwood*

*Below:* The main customer – of two – for the Dennis Domino was Greater Manchester PTE, which bought 20 (South Yorkshire bought 14) – with Northern Counties 24-seat bodies. *Stewart J. Brown*

# Municipal Muddles

At one time there were around 100 municipal bus operations in the UK; over the years the number has dropped dramatically. Thirty-four disappeared into the new PTEs in the 1960s/1970s. Others grouped with neighbours following local government reorganisation, while others still chose to sell out to bigger groups. Like the NBC sell-off, there were municipal companies that briefly went to management teams before being sold off again. Some – and the number seems to reduce every year – remain in local authority ownership.

A few suffered more ignominious fates.

**MERTHYR** Corporation began operating buses in 1924 and Merthyr Tydfil Transport was set up as the council's arm's-length company in 1986, but its financial health gradually deteriorated and the council offered the company for sale. It was bought by a consortium of local independent operators, but competition with National Welsh weakened its position and in July 1989 the administrators were called in. The company ceased trading the following month.

**MAIDSTONE** Corporation ran trams from 1904 to 1930, trolleybuses from 1928 to 1967 and motorbuses from 1924. In 1986 the newly formed Maidstone Borough Transport adopted a new livery and the fleetname Boro'line for its 40-bus fleet, which quickly moved away from its domination by Bedfords. It also had ambitions beyond Maidstone and in 1988 won London Transport tenders that first took it into the Bexley area and then into central London. This meant that the fleet had to grow and by 1990 it totalled almost 130 buses and coaches. And it was losing money.

Although Boro'line was put up for sale in 1991, its privatised neighbour, Maidstone & District, registered a competing network in Maidstone pushing Boro'line into administrative receivership early in 1992. In a few months it was all over, with M&D buying its assets, including buses and the garage. Boro'line's downfall was probably the speed of its expansion.

**LANCASTER** Corporation had operated trams from 1903 to 1930 and buses from 1916 and in 1974 merged with Morecambe & Heysham to form Lancaster District, with the

Merthyr Tydfil famously bought a batch of 13 Leyland Lynx in 1987, but these were not enough to secure the future of the company. *Stephen Morris*

buses from the two undertakings operating as Lancaster City Transport. In 1993 LCT was put up for sale, but Stagecoach moved in and registered services over most of LCT's routes; it then engineered a deal with the council to acquire the depot and some buses, incorporating the LCT services into the Ribble network. The Competition Commission regarded the move as a merger against the public interest and placed restrictions on Stagecoach's ability to retaliate against any new entrants into the market by reduced fares or increased frequencies. In the event, there was no competition.

**DARLINGTON** Corporation operated trams from 1902 to 1926, trolleybuses from 1926 to 1957 and motorbuses from 1950. The arm's-length Darlington Transport Company was formed in 1986, but although it attempted some expansion it was also facing competition from United Auto and Your Bus.

In 1994 Darlington council decided to sell its bus company and Yorkshire Traction emerged as the preferred bidder. But before it could take control, Stagecoach's Busways company registered a network of town services and tried to attract Darlington drivers to join its new Stagecoach Darlington operation with a financial inducement. Yorkshire Traction quickly withdrew from the scene and Darlington Transport went into administration. The town settled down to

competition between two main players, Stagecoach and United (eventually absorbed into Arriva), though there was an unexpected twist in 2007 when Arriva North East announced a deal to acquire the Stagecoach Darlington business.

**CHESTER** Corporation ran trams between 1902 and 1930, then buses right through to 2007. It had been known since 2006 that Chester City Council wanted to sell its bus operation, and that Arriva, keen to buy it to integrate the city routes with its out-of-town services, was frustrated by lack of progress with the sale. Arriva had registered the entire ChesterBus commercial network in September 2006, to start operations in January 2007, and offered to buy the undertaking. The council refused and Arriva submitted revised registrations for two of the ChesterBus routes. A legal challenge was raised by the council, alleging that Arriva's actions were anti-competitive. This was rejected and Arriva launched new Chester Citybus services at the same time as First was confirmed as the successful bidder for ChesterBus, by now severely devalued by the events of the previous year.

Maidstone Boro'line may have over-extended itself when it took on London Buses contracts, here on the 188 using an ex-Nottingham Daimler Fleetline. *R. J. Waterhouse*

Lancaster City Transport invested in second-hand buses in its final years. This is one of three former GM Buses Volvo Ailsa/Northern Counties bought in 1981. *M. Fowler*

A reminder of happier days in Chester: a corporation Guy Arab IV/Massey still in use in 1974. *A. Moyes*

# Worth a Try

It was Midland Red that really showed bus and coach operators that an underfloor-engined chassis was a practical proposition. Although AEC and Leyland had done some work on horizontal engines before World War II, and Sentinel had unexpectedly shown a production vehicle in 1948 while it was still work in progress for the big boys, Midland Red had introduced its own-make underfloor-engined BMMO S6 in 1946 and had hundreds in service by the time other manufacturers were still finalising their new models.

The market leaders – AEC, Bristol, Daimler, Guy and Leyland – all enjoyed success with their underfloor-engined models when they eventually got them into production.

But there were other manufacturers keen to break into the bus market who saw the potential in competing

Sentinel and Beadle combined to give the bus manufacturing industry a fright with the STC4 underfloor-engined model – perhaps frightening Leyland most, as its local operator, Ribble, bought batches.

*Above:* Midland Red had substantial numbers of its underfloor-engined S6 model in service before the major manufacturers caught up. These S6s were photographed in 1947.

Silent reliable power

Sentinel BUSES AND COACHES

SENTINEL (Shrewsbury) LIMITED, SHREWSBURY    Telephone : Shrewsbury 3811    Telegrams : Sentinol, Shrewsbury

*Left:* A Sentinel STC4 for Dicksons, Dundee, is featured in this 1952 advert against the background of the Forth Bridge, presumably on the basis that the customer was Scottish.

models, particularly as a relaxation in length regulations for single-deckers permitted 30ft-long vehicles, increasing the seating capacity to a useful 44/45 on buses and typically 41 on coaches.

Albion developed a bus chassis, the KP71NW, one of a series of experimental models developed around the KP engine series. The KP71NW had a horizontal 8-cylinder engine and two were built with Scottish Aviation bodies. The first, in 1952, was a bus that went to Glasgow Corporation, the second a coach that went to Western SMT. The KP71NW was effectively dead in the water, as Leyland had bought Albion in 1951 and decided that the company's efforts should be focused in other directions. Albion would return to the underfloor single-deck market in 1957 with the Aberdonian MR11, which enjoyed some success as a lighter and simpler alternative to Leyland's Tiger Cub.

Atkinson had built its business on Gardner-engined trucks and identified a niche market for a Gardner underfloor-engined bus and coach chassis. Initially there wasn't anything on the open market to satisfy this demand.

*Right:* A 1950 artist's impression of the ill-fated Dennis Dominant bus.

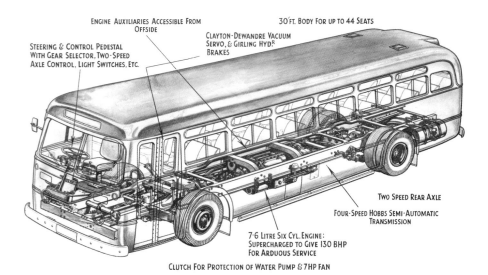

ENGINE AUXILIARIES ACCESSIBLE FROM OFFSIDE

30'FT. BODY FOR UP TO 44 SEATS

CLAYTON-DEWANDRE VACUUM SERVO, & GIRLING HYD.R BRAKES

STEERING & CONTROL PEDESTAL WITH GEAR SELECTOR, TWO-SPEED AXLE CONTROL, LIGHT SWITCHES, ETC.

TWO SPEED REAR AXLE

FOUR-SPEED HOBBS SEMI-AUTOMATIC TRANSMISSION

7·6 LITRE SIX CYL. ENGINE: SUPERCHARGED TO GIVE 130 BHP FOR ARDUOUS SERVICE

CLUTCH FOR PROTECTION OF WATER PUMP & 7HP FAN

*Right:* Dennis didn't give up and bounced back with the lighter-weight Pelican. This was the only one built, with a Duple body.

*Below:* The Dennis Lancet UF was more successful than the Dominant or Pelican, but it hardly set the world on fire. This is one of eight delivered to Newport Corporation in 1956 with unusual D. J. Davies 42-seat rear-entrance bodies. *Gavin Booth*

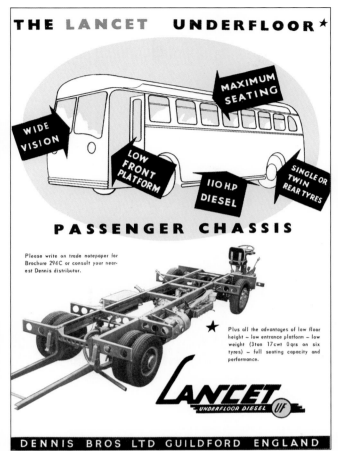

THE LANCET UNDERFLOOR ★

WIDE VISION

MAXIMUM SEATING

LOW FRONT PLATFORM

110 H.P DIESEL

SINGLE OR TWIN REAR TYRES

PASSENGER CHASSIS

Please write on trade notepaper for Brochure 294C or consult your nearest Dennis distributor.

★ Plus all the advantages of low floor height – low entrance platform – low weight (3ton 17cwt 0qrs on six tyres) – full seating capacity and performance.

LANCET UNDERFLOOR DIESEL UF

DENNIS BROS LTD GUILDFORD ENGLAND

Bristols were only available to the state sector, and when Daimler and Guy introduced their underfloor models, these were sturdy chassis with Gardner's big 6HLW engine. Guy quickly introduced a lighter chassis with the 5HLW engine, but Atkinson was there too with its Alpha PM745H with 5HLW engine, the first examples going to North Western in 1952. This was followed by the bigger-engined PM746H (6HLW) and even-smaller-engined PL744 (4HLW), but most support for the Walton-le-Dale, Preston-based company came from operators in the north-west of England; Lancashire United and North Western took just over half of the 117 chassis built between 1950 and 1963.

Beadle of Dartford made a name for itself in the late 1940s rebuilding pre-war buses for larger operators and in conjunction with Sentinel bodied the first commercially available underfloor-engined buses from 1948. Although only 58 of these were built, with most going to smaller operators, Sentinel also produced separate chassis that were sold to operators in the early 1950s. Beadle bounced back with integral bus and coach models using the remarkable and noisy Commer TS3 two-stroke engine, building 141 between 1954 and 1957, sold mainly to larger operators.

*Left:* A 1952 trade advert for the Dennis Lancet UF draws attention to its main features and highlights a low chassis weight of 3ton 17cwt.

*Below:* Atkinson was one of the truck-makers who tried their hand with bus chassis. This lightweight bus – note the single rear wheels – has a Burlingham body.

Atkinson attracted some faithful customers, including Venture of Consett, which bought several batches between 1955 and 1958. This is a 1957 Alpha BPL745H with Willowbrook 45-seat body.

Dennis, which by the 1990s had become Britain's major bus chassis builder after a number of false starts, also dabbled in the underfloor-engined single-deck market in the early 1950s. It first built the Dominant, in 1950, a chassis with a horizontal Dennis O.6 7.58-litre engine, a turbocharger and a Hobbs automatic gearbox; one was built. Then it introduced the Lancet UF, a lighter and simpler chassis using the same engine, and this enjoyed some success. Then it developed the Pelican, a lightweight chassis with a 5.5-litre engine, and although this proved successful in service, only one was built.

Seddon, like Atkinson, was a truck builder nibbling at the bus market and among models introduced in the 1950s was the Pennine Mark 11 with a *vertical* Perkins R6 engine mounted amidships. Although this was a fairly compact unit, it still resulted in a high floor line. Seddon's success in the home bus market was limited until the

appearance of the RU rear-engined bus in 1969, the front-engined Pennine 4.236 Midi in 1972 and the underfloor-engined Pennine VII in 1973.

Three more chassis builders who tried their hand in the 1950s in rather different ways were Foden, Rowe and Rutland. Foden and Rutland decided that rear engines were the answer with their PVR and Clipper models; with 54 sales, mainly for coaching work, the Foden PVR outsold Rutland's Croydon-built Clipper, which only managed three. Rowe was a Cornish coach operator that developed the Meadows-engined Hillmaster model in 1953, with underfloor-mounted engine, but few were built.

If there is a message from this, it's about giving customers something they are comfortable with. For many, moving to these newfangled underfloor-engined buses in the early 1950s was enough of a jump without throwing new engines and gearboxes into the mix. Bus company engineers are often fairly conservative souls and are more likely to be won over by buses that include familiar components. Give them a Gardner, an AEC or a Leyland engine, and they will be happy. Or at least as happy as engineers can be.

Atkinson's underfloor-engined chassis were built in fits and starts for several years. A 1963 Sunderland Corporation Alpha BPL746H with two-door Marshall body features in this 1964 advert.

# United is Untied

The very name of the company – British Electric Traction – provided a clue to its origins. BET was set up in 1895 and was all about taking over tramways to electrify them, setting up new tramway systems and creating electricity-generating concerns. It started dabbling in newfangled motorbuses at an early stage and worked closely with Tilling, itself a growing bus group. Tilling and BET went their separate ways in 1942, and by this time many of the bus companies had substantial railway shareholdings. These helped to lead Tilling into state ownership in 1948, but BET Group remained staunchly independent of state control and expanded its business with bus companies overseas, as well as into such diverse fields as TV rental, relay and broadcasting, freight transport and construction.

By the 1960s BET Group's UK bus interests were showing a poor net return and with change in the air it decided to sell them to the state-controlled Transport Holding Company in 1967, paving the way for the creation of National Bus Company in 1969.

Rivals in Manchester – Sherpas from the Ribble (front) and United Transport Bee Line Buzz Company fleets turn into Piccadilly in June 1988. Ribble would acquire the Bee Line Buzz operation the following month.

All of which set the scene for BET's unexpected return to the UK bus scene nearly 20 years later, just as NBC was being broken up and sold off into private ownership.

In 1986 minibuses were seen as one way that bus companies could run competitively, and most of the major UK fleets dabbled with smaller buses to some extent. There were new entrants to the market, nibbling at the edges and sometimes giving established operators a good run for their money.

But there was one threat that every operator took seriously. United Transport, part of the BET Group, announced that it would be introducing 250 minibuses to routes in Manchester and West Yorkshire. Half a dozen Transits could be dealt with, but this posed a serious threat to operators who were often struggling at the same time to buy their companies from NBC. United was known to have ordered at least 125 Carlyle-bodied Freight Rover Sherpas and 50 Northern Counties-bodied Dodges, and with the financial clout of BET behind these operations, the whole industry sat up to take notice. The implication was that the 250 minibuses were just the start.

United started running in the Altrincham and Stockport areas of Greater Manchester in January 1987, trading as Bee Line Buzz Company; its buses were painted yellow with a black skirt and red roof, with a bee as its logo. It used 175 18-seat Carlyle-bodied Sherpas and 50 Northern Counties-bodied 22-seat Dodge S46s.

The incumbent operators fought back, notably GM Buses which launched its own minibus operation, Little Gems, using Northern Counties Dodges, Robin Hood-bodied Iveco-Fords and MCW Metroriders.

A quick response was important in these early days of deregulation and the first Little Gems entered service in February. A similarly prompt response by Yorkshire Rider brought minibuses to the streets of Leeds before United Transport could start, and it seems that may have been enough to warn it off.

So United turned its attentions to Preston and in April started its Zippy operation with Iveco-Fords, Sherpas and, unusually, three-axle Talbot Pullmans. Three weeks later Preston Transport retaliated with Northern Counties-bodied Dodges.

Elsewhere in the country rumours flew around bus companies every time a piece of land was bought that had potential as a United minibus depot, but things were not going so well in Preston and it may have been that United leapt in without properly assessing the market. Late in 1986 there were rumours of a United operation in south-west England, but United Transport was destined to disappear as suddenly as it had appeared.

The management of newly privatised Ribble bought the Zippy operation in March 1988, and although United had one last try with its Manchester network with City Sprint-branded minibuses, by June the same year it announced that it was disposing of its Manchester operation. Ribble again emerged as the successful buyer, adding over 300 minibuses to its fleet.

In the 1980s BET disposed of many of its less profitable businesses and in 1996 was acquired by Rentokil, after a hostile takeover bid. The merged company was named Rentokil Initial, which incorporated the name of one of BET's core subsidiaries.

After only a year Ribble sold off the Bee Line Buzz company to Drawlane and the Bee Line livery and brand started to appear on double-deckers, like this ex-Ribble Leyland Atlantean/Park Royal in Manchester Piccadilly in 1990. *Gavin Booth*

# The Guy Who Called Wulf

uy Motors was not a serious contender in the bus business until World War II. The company had been around since 1914 building lorries and, for a while, private cars, and while in the 1920s and 1930s it built increasing numbers of bus and trolleybus chassis, it was never in the big league like AEC, Daimler or Leyland.

But then things changed dramatically.

In the early years of World War II the Ministry of Transport drew up specifications for simple and rugged buses that would help to keep the country moving during these difficult years when many materials were in short supply. Originally Guy and Leyland were each asked to build an initial batch of 500 double-deck chassis, but

Leyland's efforts were diverted to military vehicle production and by default Guy became the main supplier of double-deckers for the next few years.

The chassis it built, the Arab, was based on a model of the same name it had built between 1934 and 1939. The wartime Arab may have lacked the sophistication that operators had come to expect in the later pre-war years, but it was very welcome in fleets of all sizes throughout the UK, most of whom had no previous experience of Guy vehicles. The 1942 Arab used cast iron where its 1934 predecessor

Most Wulfrunians found their way into the West Riding fleet. This is an ex-County Roe-bodied example in 1969. *D. J. Little*

*Above:* The Wulfrunian bodied by East Lancs for West Wales in 1961, seen before delivery.

*Left:* The West Wales Wulfrunian/East Lancs also ended up with West Riding, seen here in Pontefract in 1967. *M. J. Kernick*

The only Northern Counties-bodied Wulfrunian was delivered to Lancashire United in 1960.

used aluminium and with a Gardner 5LW or 6LW engine and a double-plate clutch and sliding mesh gearbox it was a solid – almost unbreakable – piece of kit that operators grew to love. So much so that after the war it continued in production in gradually more sophisticated versions. The wartime Arabs are usually referred to as MkI and MkII models, and the last Arab, the MkV, was built in 1969. Many operators that had first met the Arab during the war stayed faithful to the type well into the post-war years.

Then came the Wulfrunian.

It came at a time when double-deck bus design was going through major changes, partly encouraged by the relaxation of length regulations to allow 30ft long buses. Leyland had amazed the industry with its rear-engined Atlantean, which went into production late in 1958, and Daimler would follow with its Gardner-engined Fleetline in 1960.

Guy chose to go down a different route. The Wulfrunian had its engine at the front, though offset towards the driver who was squeezed into a cramped area on the offside of the bus, and because the front wheels were set back behind the driver, a front-mounted entrance and platform was possible. Guy's innovation didn't stop there, though. There

was air suspension all round, still a new feature at the time. There was independent suspension at the front and a drop-centre double reduction rear axle. And four-wheel disc brakes, the first on a bus.

Guy had been encouraged to develop the Wulfrunian by the West Riding company, still an independent at the time, and West Riding would go on to take 126 of the 137 Wulfrunians built.

Roe built the bodies on the two prototypes used as demonstrators and also on Wulfrunians for Bury Corporation (1) and County Motors (2). East Lancs bodied the Accrington (2), West Wales (1) and Wolverhampton (2) examples, while Northern Counties built just one, for Lancashire United.

The only trouble was – it was a disaster. It quickly gained a reputation for unreliability and its advanced features proved to be more trouble than they were worth. The Wulfrunian rode badly on the uneven roads that characterised West Riding's patch in the coal-mining belt to the south of Leeds, centred on Wakefield. Although a few staunch Guy customers bought Wulfrunians, they quickly regretted it and County, Lancashire United and West Wales unloaded their examples on West Riding.

Modified Wulfrunians were delivered to Accrington, which bought two in 1961, and to Wolverhampton in 1962. Wolverhampton, supporting local industry, had bought a standard Wulfrunian in 1961, but its second, in 1962, was, with Accrington's two, a slightly different beast. The engine was centrally mounted at the front and there was a shorter front overhang as the entrance position was not to be at the extreme front. All three had East Lancs bodies, the Accrington buses had rear entrances and the Wolverhampton bus had a forward entrance, behind the front axle. Even in this modified form the Wulfrunian suffered from mechanical and suspension problems.

The Wulfrunian was bad news for both Guy and West Riding. Development of such an advanced model was costly and the limited sales did not allow Guy to recoup its costs; this was aggravated by mounting warranty claims. On top of all this, Guy was suffering from an ill-advised expansion into South Africa and the company was ripe for acquisition. Although Leyland had sniffed around, it was Jaguar that made the move. It had already bought car and bus builder Daimler, in 1960, and in 1961 bought the fast-failing Guy Motors. Five years later Jaguar merged with British Motor Corporation, builders of Austin and Morris cars, to form British Motor Holdings, but BMH was to be short-lived. Leyland had started its serious empire-building in 1962 when it acquired AEC, along with bodybuilders Park Royal and Roe, and over the decade mopped up car makers Standard-Triumph and Rover, along with bus builders Bristol and ECW. In 1968 Leyland bid for BMH, creating the British Leyland giant, which was probably a step too far, as events in the 1970s and 1980s would prove. But in the short term it sounded the death-knell for quite a few famous names, Guy included.

West Riding, which had not only built up a substantial fleet of Wulfrunians but also bought Daimler Roadliners, was sufficiently weakened to sell out to the Transport Holding Company in 1967, passing into the new National Bus Company in 1969.

## WULFRUNIAN CUSTOMERS

| | | | |
|---|---|---|---|
| West Riding | 126 | Roe-bodied | 1959-1965 |
| Accrington | 2 | East Lancs-bodied | 1961 |
| County | 2 | Roe-bodied | 1960 |
| Wolverhampton | 2 | East Lancs-bodied | 1960/62 |
| Bury | 1 | Roe-bodied | 1960 |
| Lancashire United | 1 | Northern Counties-bodied | 1960 |
| West Wales | 1 | East Lancs-bodied | 1961 |
| Demonstrators | 2 | Roe-bodied | 1960 |
| *TOTAL* | *137* | | |

Accrington's Wulfrunians combined its advanced features with a more traditional rear-entrance East Lancs body, as seen in 1962. *G. R. Mills*

*Above:* A similar bus, also East Lancs-bodied but with a forward entrance, was built for Wolverhampton Corporation. *M. J. Fenton*

*Right:* The bus that started it all, West Riding no 863, the 1959 prototype Wulfrunian with Roe body for West Riding, and the only one with this particular style of front-end treatment.

# Ahead of His Time?

Norman Morton was just 42 when he became general manager and engineer of Sunderland Corporation Transport Department in 1952. In those days municipal managers worked their way up the ladder and most tended to be rather older than Morton when they took up their posts.

He quickly made his mark at Sunderland, accelerating the tramway withdrawal programme, introducing route numbers on the buses, redesigning the bus stop signs and modernising the fleet numbers and lettering on his buses.

Morton was a bit of a visionary and wrote discussion papers on a wide range of transport topics. But he was not afraid to test his ideas out in Sunderland. He converted older buses for driver-only operation for use on a colliery night shift service and charged a flat 6d fare. Others were converted for a loss-making service with a flat fare of 2d; passengers could buy books of 12 vouchers for 1s 9d.

Faced with declining passenger numbers and increasing costs in the 1960s he advocated the adoption of a flat fare

An earlier Norman Morton innovation was this lightweight Atkinson with 41-seat Roe body, delivered in 1956. He was looking for a front-engined lightweight one-man-operated bus that was cheaper to buy and run than underfloor-engined single-deckers.

for all Sunderland Corporation passengers, irrespective of the journey length. He had seen Copenhagen's driver-only flat fare token-operated system and liked what he saw.

His grand plan for Sunderland was to replace the fleet with large-capacity driver-only standee single-deckers over a four-year period and introduce a 4d flat fare across the system. The buses started to arrive in 1966, fitted with Autoslot token-operated ticket machines – for Morton had decided to go the whole hog and introduce tokens too.

Passengers could buy tokens at 10 for 2s 9d (representing a 21 per cent saving), but cash passengers were still accommodated. On the new single-deckers token-carrying passengers entered the right side of the front entrance and placed a token in the ticket machine to obtain a ticket. Other passengers used the left side and paid the driver in cash or bought tokens from the driver.

It was a brave move, but at a time of rising costs Morton was forced to apply for a rise in the flat fare. However, a change of political party in the council brought a sudden end to the flat fare scheme, and it was announced that a zonal scheme would be introduced with a token paying for each section.

This was too much for Norman Morton, who resigned in 1967 and went into transport research. Although passenger receipts had increased greatly in his 15 years at Sunderland, a profit had turned into a serious deficit and passenger numbers were way down.

Although tokens for bus journeys have been tried by other operators with varying degrees of success, flat fares have proved successful in various city fleets, notably Brighton & Hove, Lothian (Edinburgh) and in London, and there has been a massive swing towards off-bus ticketing, with, in the case of Edinburgh and London at least, pavement-mounted ticket machines.

Maybe 1960s Sunderland was not ready for tokens and flat fares, but someone has to try these things, even if only to prove that they don't work. Sunderland Corporation survived as an entity until 1973 when it was merged with Tyneside PTE in advance of the creation of Tyne & Wear PTE in 1974.

*Above:* The single-deckers ordered for the token experiments had distinctively styled two-door bodies and were mounted on a range of chassis – AEC Swift, Bristol RE, Daimler Roadliner and Leyland Panther. This is a Panther/Strachans. *G. Coxon*

*Right:* Norman Morton came up with a unique body style for his driver-only single-deckers with forward-sloping window pillars.

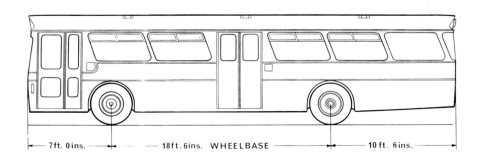

7ft. 0ins.     18ft. 6ins. WHEELBASE     10ft. 6ins.

# A Deck Too Far?

It makes economic sense to cram as many people on to a bus or coach as can comfortably be carried. The passengers' view of 'comfortably' may of course differ from the operator's.

For years 35 was probably the comfortable seating limit in coaches that were almost invariably front-engined, single-deck and 27ft 6in long. Underfloor-engined coaches in the 1950s allowed coaches with seats for up to 41 passengers, and when coaches grew to 36ft long that number increased to 49 or 51. Operators had to wait until 1961 for such high capacities, so some looked at other ways of gaining capacity.

Ribble saw a role for double-deck coaches – and in fairness it kept returning to this theme. Its first were the White Ladies, built on Leyland Titan PD1/3 chassis in 1948 by Burlingham, with heavily chromed full fronts, coach seats and such 'luxury' touches as Perspex sliding roofs on the upper deck. There were 10 of these followed by 20 similar buses, but Titan PD2/3s with East Lancs bodies. The White Ladies were used on Ribble's longer-distance services in the north-west of England, but by 1956 the buses were being painted red for normal service work.

The double-deck coach theme was revisited in 1959 when Ribble unveiled its new Weymann-bodied Leyland Atlantean 50-seat coach to coincide with the opening of the first parts of Britain's motorway system. The coaches, labelled Gay Hostesses, were used on Ribble's services linking the north-west with London, run jointly with its associated Standerwick and Scout fleets. A new generation of White Ladies appeared in 1962, more normal Atlantean/Weymanns with 59 seats, for use on medium-distance routes.

The next generation from Ribble represented a significant step forward. This was the 1968 Bristol VRL with 36ft-long ECW bodywork for 60. And a total of 30 would be delivered by 1972. These were undoubtedly impressive coaches – to look at and sit in, at least – but reliability problems plus concerns about stability after one overturned on a motorway journey affected their success.

A 1961 Ribble photo shows a stewardess serving tea on the upper deck of one of the Standerwick Gay Hostess Atlanteans. The original caption tells us: 'Gay Hostess is truly hospitable for provision is made for the serving of light refreshments – sandwiches, cakes, biscuits, chocolates and sweets etc, tea and orange juice. Sales on coaches have been averaging 25,000 items a vehicle a year.' The caption adds that 'refreshments may be eaten whilst the coach continues on its journey'.

*Above:* Two of Standerwick's Bristol VRTL/ECW coaches pick up passengers at Coventry in 1971. *T. W. Moore*

*Right:* Leyland's prototype double-deck Olympian coach received an ECW body that was all too clearly a bus body with a different front end. Later examples would be more attractive. *M. S. Curtis*

This was a pity because the world would be ready for double-deck coaches in a few years' time, when express coach services were deregulated in 1980. In this brave new world operators were looking for extra capacity to keep fares down, but unfortunately no British manufacturers had a suitable model on their lists. This gave European builders like Neoplan and, to a lesser degree, Van Hool the chance to sell to British operators, but as we can see elsewhere in this book, MCW quickly put the Metroliner together. Leyland also wanted in on the act, but its double-deck coaches were not 'pure' coaches, tending to be longer versions of its standard Leyland/ECW Olympian model, designed mostly for commuter-type services.

After Leyland and MCW had disappeared Neoplan and Van Hool continued to supply double-deck express coaches in small numbers, and there was a limited market for double-deck touring coaches, particularly for shuttle services to southern Europe.

Stagecoach had been an early user of Neoplan double-deckers on its express services and returned to Neoplan for Skyliner coaches for its low-cost Megabus operation as well as its high-profile Oxford Tube service, but the Megabus vehicles were rather overtaken by the relaxation of regulations that allowed 15m-long coaches, leading to a move to 63-seat single-deck coaches. This may have been hastened by a 2007 accident involving a National Express Skyliner.

Stagecoach has also explored articulated single-deck coaches as a means of achieving high seating capacity, but these have settled on medium-distance routes.

Although there have been a few accidents involving double-deck coaches, the vehicle itself has rarely been to blame. Nonetheless the story of double-deck coaches for express services in Britain has not been a happy one.

*Left:* The Leyland Olympian with ECW coach bodies for NBC companies were essentially lengthened buses with coach seats and other trimmings, and with a more streamlined front end. Most, like this Eastern National 1984 example, were used on commuter journeys.

*Below:* Leyland latterly reworked its Olympian/ECW to produce something that looked more coach-like.

*Above:* Scottish Bus Group turned to Alexander to produce four double-deck coaches based on the R type structure. This was one of two built on Volvo Citybus chassis for Fife Scottish.

*Right:* In sales terms, the MCW Metroliner was the most successful of the British-built double-deck coaches, with National Bus Company and Scottish Bus Group each taking deliveries for use on longer-distance motorway journeys.

# Not Invented Here

Nobody can deny that London and the needs of Londoners have played a part in bus design for the best part of a century. Double-deck bus design in particular has been influenced by London, which has always been the largest market and therefore concentrated the minds of manufacturers who wanted to count London companies among their customers.

AEC, set up as an in-house chassis builder for the London General company in 1912, supplied most of London's needs under the direction of London General, and even after AEC was floated off as a separate business when London Transport was formed in 1933 it had the cushion of an agreement to supply not less than 90 per cent of London Transport's motorbus chassis over the next dozen years. This situation would continue after World War II, which was fine for AEC and later its associated

The two best-known – and probably best-loved – of London's own-design buses are the RT (right) and Routemaster. For 50 years from the late 1940s these two types, individually and collectively, would dominate the London bus fleet, hardly surprising when you recall that nearly 10,000 buses of the RT and RM families were built.

bodybuilder, Park Royal, but was frustrating for other builders, notably Leyland, that, not unreasonably, wanted a slice of the London market. Leyland did manage to become a major trolleybus supplier to LT and also built some Londonised versions of its staple products, like the Titan-based STDs; Leyland was also used for experimental single-deck work, like the underfloor-engined TF type Tigers and the rear-engined CR type Cubs.

Leyland had to fall in line to retain LT business after World War II, and its rewards were the orders for the RTL and RTW types, heavily adapted versions of its Titan PD2 chassis, although it didn't get a look in when LT was ordering its big post-war single-deck class, which materialised as the AEC-built RF type.

Leyland was given the chance to build two prototypes of the LT-designed Routemaster, although its involvement in the production version was restricted to the supply of engines for around 20 per cent of London's 2,760 Routemasters.

Although the Routemaster gained iconic status, particularly after the last RTs ran in service, it was not without its troubles in the early days. There were problems with its brakes, gearbox, steering column, suspension, rear axle and main A and B frames, according to Ken Blacker's definitive book 'Routemaster'. 'In its early days,' he wrote, 'the Routemaster was, without doubt, an engineer's nightmare.' Overheating was a big problem and an RM was gutted by a flywheel fire in 1966.

Apart from a last-ditch effort to prove how versatile the Routemaster was by designing a rear-engined version, the FRM, by the late 1960s the heady days of London-designed buses were over. Well, almost.

While it is true that there would never be another 100 per cent London-designed bus, manufacturers would be expected to design new models with more than half an eye

# ROUTEMASTER

In the last 100 years London's streets have seen a fine variety of shapes and sizes of bus. Each successive type has been evolved in the light of experience gained, each has taken advantage of technical advances.

The present bus in this honourable succession is the familiar post-war RT, and the 6,600 buses of this type now on London's streets have many more years of good service yet to give. But the time needed to get a new bus into quantity production makes it imperative to look ahead. Engineers at London Transport's Chiswick Works have related London's present-day transport needs and traffic conditions to the experience gained with the RT bus, and the result is the ROUTE-MASTER, the prototype of the London bus of the future, which recently went into experimental service on Route 2 between Golders Green and Crystal Palace.

Although it is in appearance not unlike its predecessor, the Routemaster is revolutionary in construction. It is built of aluminium alloy as an immensely strong box, without a conventional chassis. The resultant saving of weight will in its turn save fuel. Riding is smoother and quieter than anything Londoners have previously known. The gangways are wider and as passengers pass on or off the bus the conductor can stand out of the way in an alcove under the stairs. Electric-hydraulic gear changing makes the new bus as easy to drive as a modern car. And there are 64 seats as against the present 56.

It will be some years before the Routemaster becomes a familiar part of the London scene — years, perhaps, of modification and improvement. Meanwhile, if you happen to meet its prototype and have any comments on its suitability and efficiency, please write to the Public Relations Officer, 55 Broadway, S.W.1.

*MAKE THE MOST OF YOUR PUBLIC TRANSPORT*

on London's needs, or would need to produce heavily modified versions of their normal types.

The growth of what would become British Leyland in 1968 meant that most of LT's suppliers were now in single ownership. This may explain why the FRM was never allowed to develop, given that BL had models like the Atlantean and Fleetline, each with years of 'provincial' service under their belts.

So LT, possibly reluctantly, placed orders for batches of experimental types – 50 Leyland Atlanteans and eight Daimler Fleetlines with (deliberately?) plain-looking Park Royal bodies, and 15 of AEC's new rear-engined Swift, so heavily Londonised they were referred to as Merlins. Almost before these had a chance to prove themselves, LT ordered bewilderingly large numbers of Merlins and Swifts, quickly got rid of the Atlanteans and ordered the first of a large fleet of Daimler Fleetlines.

The Merlins and Swifts proved embarrassingly troublesome, and withdrawal of the 665 Merlins that had been delivered between 1966 and 1969 started in 1974; there were 838 Swifts delivered between 1969 and 1972, and withdrawal of these started in 1976. While many were sold for further service overseas, few entered service in the UK.

The Fleetlines too had their problems. A total of 2,646 were delivered between 1970 and 1978, but by 1976 LT was admitting that the type had not proved a complete success in London and no more would be ordered. Barely had the last Fleetlines entered service in 1978 than LT decided that it would dispose of the fleet in favour of Leyland Titans and MCW Metrobuses. Withdrawals started in 1979, with some going for scrap and others finding ready customers in the UK and abroad, where they went on to give years of good service in such different yet demanding environments as Birmingham and Hong Kong.

The London argument was that these types were withdrawn because they were not suited to the arduous conditions there – something, perhaps, that should have been established before such large orders were placed. There is also the suggestion that they suffered from the Not Invented Here syndrome and that engineers would rather fix a Routemaster than a Fleetline.

The Forward entrance, PARK ROYAL ROUTE-MASTER in Service with Northern General Transport Company Limited.

PARK ROYAL – ROE
*Sales Division*

HEAD OFFICE AT:
PARK ROYAL VEHICLES LTD
ABBEY ROAD, LONDON, N.W. 10
TELEPHONE: ELGAR 6522 (10 LINES)    TELEGRAMS: KOACHWORKS HARLES, LONDON
PRV    ROE

*Above left and left:*
Although Park Royal worked hard to promote the Routemaster to other operators, Northern General was the only operator outside London to buy the type new.

*Right:* One of the 50 short-lived Leyland Atlantean/Park Royals bought by London Transport, in Whitehall in 1965.
*Victor C. K. Allen*

*Below right:* One of the London Atlanteans is featured in a 1970 leaflet announcing experimental flat-fare buses in the Peckham area.

Whatever the situation, LT's post-Routemaster buying policies were disastrous and clearly something better was needed for the next generation. Leyland was the UK's dominant bus builder and worked with LT to produce the integral B15 double-deck, which went into production as the Titan TN15. Although its future was threatened at several stages by Leyland's internal problems, 1,125 were built for London and widely acknowledged to be good buses. Few non-London Titans were built, but London's second-hand Titans were quickly snapped up. MCW had developed the Metrobus with London and West Midlands orders in mind and this model also turned out to work well in London.

But even while London Transport was working with Leyland on the B15 project, LT engineers were beavering away at a project of their own – the XRM. This would have a side-mounted engine, small wheels to give a flatter floor, and a hydraulic drive system. It would be 9.5m long with up to 67 seats in a single-door layout.

The low floor would be achieved with small wheels, eight of them, an idea that had been explored before in the Moulton super-coach and Leyland Commutabus projects. LT bought a Bedford VAL, the twin-steer six-wheel single-deck chassis that had been popular in the 1960s and 1970s, but possible problems with tyre wear and scrub, and braking, led to the abandonment of the multi-axle concept. Problems too were experienced with an experimental hydraulic drive system and in 1978 the eight-wheel concept was abandoned and a more conventional two-axle bus – still with a side-mounted engine – was considered. But this too bit the dust when the XRM project ceased in 1980. By this time the Metrobuses and Titans had bedded in and were giving satisfactory service.

**STARTING JANUARY 24**

**Flat-Fare Buses**

**FOR THE PECKHAM AND NUNHEAD AREAS**

To update the single-deck fleet LT turned to the National, Leyland's mass-produced integral model, and bought over 500 between 1973 and 1981.

Since that time London has bought largely off-the-shelf types like the Leyland/Volvo Olympian and has helped to drive the UK-wide move to low-floor easy-access buses.

In the background, though, the desire to have something as successful as the Routemaster has never gone away. Every few years manufacturers would be encouraged to produce design exercises for a 'new generation' Routemaster, and often design exercises were all that these were. In the late 1980s London Buses even invited manufacturers to design a new-generation Routemaster, still with a front engine and an open rear platform, even though this was a concept that had been overtaken by fashion and events. Alexander, Dennis and Northern Counties – at that time all quite separate businesses – all showed an interest, which was not surprising if the carrot was London bus orders. What they produced were essentially Routemasters as they would appear more than 35 years after the prototype appeared. Nothing came of these.

There was also an attempt to sell the idea of a side-engined Routemaster replacement, the QRM, led by Colin Curtis, who was involved in the design of the 1950s version.

And just when it all seemed to have gone quiet, Boris Johnson replaced Ken Livingstone as Mayor of London, vowing to get rid of 'dangerous' articulated buses and launching a public competition to design a Routemaster for the 21st century – or rather, two competitions. One invited design concepts from children, the other offered a £25,000 prize for serious designs for a two- or three-axle double-deck up to 13.5m long with a minimum of 72 seats, and two entrances – one an open rear platform.

The new bus, it was said, would enter service in 2012, but of course the prize is not £25,000 but serious money if the project goes ahead.

Although most bus industry observers have been scornful of the safety implications of a new open-platform bus, manufacturers have been less dismissive and have indicated that they are taking the project seriously, which takes us back to where we started: the importance of London orders to the survival of the major suppliers to the London market. One manufacturer did make the anonymous comment: 'The original Routemaster was such a wonderful design that only one operator outside London bought it.'

The rear-engined Routemaster could have found a market outside London, but British Leyland wanted to sell its own products so this bus, FRM1, remained unique. It used a high proportion of standard Routemaster parts, which made economic sense but resulted in a bus that looked rather staid alongside its provincial contemporaries.

*Above:* The experimental London AEC Merlins had Strachans bodies and were used on the pioneering Red Arrow service.

*Right:* The Red Arrows pioneered the use of turnstiles in flat-fare buses. Passengers inserted their 6d (2.5p) in the slot to release the turnstile, and could obtain change from the machine on the right, leaving the driver free to drive the bus. Seats were provided for only 25 passengers, towards the rear of the bus, with standing space in the centre for a further 48. London passengers, used to all-seated double-deckers, were slow to adjust to this arrangement.

*Above:* Although the LT Merlins and Swifts were heavily Londonised versions of AEC's basic chassis, their stay in London was scandalously short. A Merlin/Metro-Cammell is seen on the pioneering 500 Red Arrow service when new.

*Left:* Although it was launched with a fanfare at the 1970 Commercial Motor Show, the DMS type Daimler Fleetline was destined for a short and troubled life in London – these DMSs had reached the end of the road (here at Ensign premises at Purfleet) by 1984.

*Below:* The London Fleetlines were enthusiastically snapped up by operators of all sizes in the UK and overseas. This one is running for OK, Bishop Auckland.

*Above:* Although the Leyland Titan TN15, designed with London very much in mind, enjoyed a successful career in London, very few were sold to other operators; Reading Transport bought 12 between 1979 and 1983. Most operators ignored the Titan and chose Leyland's Olympian instead.

*Right:* Late in the Routemaster's London life an extensive refurbishment programme was launched to extend the lives of the remaining 500 examples. The process involved re-engining and a complete body overhaul with new seat fabric, red handpoles and new fluorescent lighting. The effect was attractive, and bought the buses another ten years in service. When TfL replaced London Transport in 2000 a similar effort took place on a smaller scale, involving vehicles actually bought back from preservationists and private operators, but the tide soon turned against the RM.

# How Britain Learned to Love the Integral

Historically, Britain was wedded to the concept of ordering a bus chassis from one supplier and the bodywork from another. Although it didn't necessarily make logistical sense (Highland Scottish in Inverness buying Fleetline chassis built at Leyland and Eastern Coach Works bodies from Lowestoft, or Premier Travel at Cambridge buying Reliance chassis from AEC at Southall and Y type bodies from Alexander at Falkirk), customers got the bus they wanted.

One-stop shopping was not unknown – Leyland famously built a reasonable proportion of the bodywork on its own double-deck chassis until 1954 – but the integral bus was a different animal.

The theory was that a bus could be built without a chassis as such, with the bodywork mounted directly on to an underframe that included all the mechanical units, thus providing an important part of the structural rigidity of the resulting bus.

It wasn't a new idea, even in the 1950s, but it was one that several manufacturers regarded as an excellent way to

AEC and Park Royal produced the integral Monocoach – actually a bus – but most operators went for its chassis contemporary, the Reliance. This is a Monocoach for Northern General at the 1954 Commercial Motor Show; in the right background is London Transport's prototype Routemaster, RM1.

reduce weight, increase structural strength and (important commercially) to buy complete vehicles from one source.

The trouble was, the operators didn't really agree.

Leyland's first commercially available underfloor-engined single-deck mode was the Olympic, built as an integral with MCW, and AEC placed great store by the AEC/Park Royal Monocoach. In practice, the Olympic was a huge success in export markets, but operators voted with their feet and preferred the separate chassis of the Royal Tiger and Tiger Cub with their own choice of

*Above:* Saunders-Roe, which had enjoyed success as a supplier of single-deck bodies on Leyland Tiger Cub chassis, also built an integral, badged as a Saro and fitted with a Gardner 5HLW engine. Just one was built and this was sold to Maidstone & District, which was involved in its development.

*Right:* Beadle built integrals based around the Commer TS3 engine, like this lightweight 44-seat bus for Northern General in 1955.

*Above:* Harrington also built integrals around Commer's unusual TS3 engine. This is a 1956 Contender 42-seat bus for Maidstone & District.

*Below:* The Leyland Atlantean was originally built as a lowheight integral bus, a joint venture with Metro-Cammell, but operators preferred a separate chassis and so this ground-breaking bus remained unique.

bodywork. The Monocoach too was vastly outsold by its companion chassis, the Reliance.

Some manufacturers stuck with the integral concept, like Beadle, which enjoyed reasonable success with integrals that incorporated running units from pre-war buses and later its own range of bus and coach models incorporating Commer TS3 engines.

AEC and Leyland both introduced integral double-deckers in 1956 – AEC the front-engined lowheight Bridgemaster and Leyland the rear-engined lowheight Atlantean. The Bridgemaster sold just 180, while the Atlantean was re-jigged as a separate chassis.

Interestingly, the operators who had less choice in what they could buy were embracing integral and semi-integral types. The Tilling Group's main single-deck model in the 1950s was the integral LS type; Midland Red's BMMO S14 and successive single-deck models and D9 double-decker were integrals; and of course the London Transport Routemaster was an integral design.

Leyland first used the Olympian name for a lightweight integral single-decker based on the Tiger Cub chassis. It was built between 1953 and 1958, and the only UK customers were Fishwick and Western Welsh. This is the 1953 prototype demonstrator.

But operators who were able to shop around were still resisting the attractions of integrals. Leyland kept returning to the integral concept and succeeded at last in the 1970s when it cornered the single-deck market with its integral National model – helped, of course, by the fact that it concurrently withdrew most of the competing chassis, which were now under its control anyway.

If operators had little choice with the integral National, it probably helped to reduce the resistance to the integral concept, opening the door for future models. Leyland tried to replicate the National's success with its integral Titan double-deck, but operators rebelled against its London-directed sophistication and flocked to buy Leyland's Olympian instead. MCW's integral Metrobus, again aimed at London, enjoyed considerably greater success throughout the UK.

And that's largely the way things have stayed, though Optare has made a good living out of integral buses, and Alexander Dennis and Wrightbus have flirted with complete buses, though not necessarily integrals. These days many 'chassis' are delivered as underframes and the bodybuilder builds an integrated (if not necessarily integral) body around it.

*Above:* The MCW Metrobus was probably the most successful integral double-decker, selling in substantial numbers to fleets like West Midlands PTE and London Transport. This is the MCW stand at the 1978 Commercial Motor Show with China Motor Bus (left) and West Midlands PTE Metrobuses on display.
*T. W. Moore*

*Left:* The Metrobus proved to a popular model and London, one of the target customers, bought 1,440 new MkI Metrobuses and two of the simplified MkII model, as shown here. These were used in the 1984/85 trials with other current double-deck types – Dennis Dominator, Leyland Olympian, Volvo Ailsa – but London would buy no more new Metrobuses.

# A Bridge Too Far

History has shown that the first was often the best. Certainly it was the case with lowheight double-deckers.

Early motorbuses tended to be high-built vehicles, which often meant they could operate only in urban areas where there were no railway or canal bridges. Gradually bus manufacturers recognised that passengers were looking for buses that were easier to use and so designed and produced lower-built chassis that meant that a typical double-decker with normal seating on both decks came out around 14.5ft high. For many operators this was ideal, but there were still bus companies looking for lower overall heights; these were typically fast-growing interurban or rural operators who required more seats than the 32 that most single-deckers provided.

Leyland took up the challenge when its new T range appeared in 1927 and produced the Titan TD1 with what it described as a 'lowbridge' body that was little more than 13ft high. This was achieved by a sunken upper deck gangway alongside a four-across bench seat. A lowbridge

The Bristol Lodekka was the first and probably the best of the front-engined lowheight double-deckers. This is the prototype FLF model, with one-piece sliding door; production FLFs had folding doors. 1,867 FLF Lodekkas were built between 1959 and 1968.

TD1 offered seats for 48 passengers, and the layout was quickly adopted by other bodybuilders and was supplied for the next 40 years. In truth, it wasn't the ideal solution as upper deck passengers were rather crammed in together and it wasn't easy for conductors to collect fares; it was a problem for lower deck passengers too, as the sunken gangway intruded into the ceiling and represented a danger to passengers sitting on the offside of the bus. But it allowed operators to meet the rising demand for bus travel.

Other manufacturers looked at the problem and there was the amazing double-decker built by Gilford and Wycombe in 1931 that featured a host of advanced features – front-wheel drive, integral construction, independent suspension, a diesel engine – including an overall height of just under 13ft. If this book covered pre-1950 buses in detail, then the Gilford would merit a chapter on its own.

Another lowheight bus in the 1930s was the 1935 Leyland TTL trolleybus with drop-centre rear axles and an overall height of 13.5ft. Like the Gilford, it disappeared without trace.

It was left to Bristol, better known for sturdy unbreakable buses than for innovative designs, to show how it should be done. The company passed into state ownership in 1948 along with Eastern Coach Works, and its products were restricted to other state-owned companies, which meant the Tilling and Scottish groups, London Transport and Yorkshire municipal fleets that had

*Above:* The Crossley-designed Bridgemaster achieved a flat floor leading from the rear platform, as the Bristol Lodekka had.

*Left:* Later Bridgemasters had forward entrances and rather ungainly Park Royal bodies, like this 1961

*Right:* The later rear-entrance Bridgemasters looked marginally more attractive than their forward-entrance brothers, as shown on this 1960 East Yorkshire example.

*Below right:* AEC was still using prototype Bridgemaster 9 JML – later bought by Birmingham City Transport – to promote the model, claiming that it was 'the finest all route double decker'. Poor sales suggest that operators did not agree.

a railway shareholding. The Tilling and Scottish groups operated large numbers of lowbridge double-deckers, mostly Bristol/ECW products in the case of Tilling and Leyland/Alexander products in Scotland.

Bristol's solution to the awkward lowbridge layout was a true lowheight double-deck with normal seating on both decks – the Lodekka. The first prototype appeared in 1949 and Bristol was canny enough to test it and a second 1950 prototype in service with its associated fleets before going into production with a revised version in 1953.

The low height of 13.5ft was achieved with a drop-centre rear axle, and most early Lodekkas were 60-seaters. The model went on to flat-floor F-series models with air suspension as well as longer versions, some with 78 seats.

But of course the Lodekka was not available to a number of important operators, like the BET Group, municipal and independent sectors who might otherwise have bought it. Or at least that was the thinking behind a range of 'me-too' models that quickly followed. The production numbers suggest that the manufacturers had misread the market.

AEC turned to its associated company, Crossley, which was asked to dust off plans for a lowheight air-suspension bus and this saw the light of day in 1956 as the integral Bridgemaster, initially badged as a Crossley, but quickly to become an AEC. Anything from AEC was likely to attract interest from a wide selection of customers, but little of the initial interest translated into orders. Only 180 AEC/Park Royal Bridgemasters were delivered, with BET Group companies taking nearly two-thirds of these. It was replaced by the Renown, a more conventional chassis that could be bodied by builders other than Park Royal, but only 251 were built.

Dennis followed a different route and entered into an agreement with Bristol to build the Lodekka under licence

## the finest all route double decker

Now—no need to confine low height double-deckers to bridge-restricted roads. The new, chassisless "Bridgemaster", with its Park Royal twin deck centre gangway body, has all the features and advantages of the orthodox double-decker—plus a new lightweight design and an overall height of only 13 ft. 5½ in. It is the *all route* bus of maximum capacity.

Finally developed after two years of continuous testing in practical service conditions, the A.E.C. Park Royal 'Bridgemaster' has proved economical to operate and—due to its advanced design—remarkably easy to maintain and overhaul. Among many outstanding features is the rear suspension and front independent coil suspension—both standard fittings—which make the 'Bridgemaster' superior in stability and riding comfort to any double-decker in service today.

* A.E.C. 6-cyl. 125 b.h.p. diesel engine
* Two wheelbases for 27 ft. 8 in. or 30 ft. bodies
* 68 or 76 passengers
* Front independent coil suspension. Rear air suspension.
* Inertia lock synchromesh gearbox and hydraulically-operated clutch

## A.E.C. BRIDGEMASTER
### Low height <u>and</u> orthodox seating

**A.C.V. SALES LIMITED**
A.E.C. WORKS, SOUTHALL, MIDDLESEX

as the Loline. Just 280 were built, with local operator Aldershot & District taking exactly half of these.

Leyland had a go with the Lowlander, usually badged as an Albion and built in Scotland largely from Leyland units. It was aimed at the Scottish Bus Group, a good

*Above:* The Albion Lowlander was a Scottish Bus Group-targeted product from Leyland. Several SBG fleets bought them and, in true SBG style, started transferring them within the group. This is a 1963 Northern Counties-bodied Lowlander, new to Western SMT but operating for Alexander (Fife). *Gavin Booth*

*Right:* An Albion Lowlander chassis shows the high-mounted engine and driving position, with the engine protruding into the saloon space, and the low build behind that, with the gearbox mounted on the nearside ahead of the drop-centre double reduction rear axle. Ahead of the bulkhead behind the engine the Lowlander was largely a Leyland Titan PD3, but the rest of the chassis, including the twin fuel tanks, was unique.

customer for lowbridge Leyland Titans, but also able to buy Lodekkas, which it did. In fairness, SBG did buy Lowlanders, but in much smaller quantities. Just 274 Lowlanders were built.

Between them the Bridgemaster, Renown, Loline and Lowlander amounted to fewer than 1,000 sales. More than 5,000 Lodekkas were sold.

## LOWHEIGHT DOUBLE-DECKERS

| | | |
|---|---|---|
| 1949 | Bristol Lodekka | (5,213 built to 1968) |
| 1956 | Crossley/AEC Bridgemaster | (180 built to 1963) |
| 1957 | Dennis Loline | (280 built to 1967) |
| 1961 | Albion Lowlander | (274 built to 1966) |
| 1963 | AEC Renown | (251 built to 1967) |

*Right:* Lacking a photo of a finished bus, Dennis used a photo of a standard Bristol/ECW Lodekka, doctored to feature a Dennis front grille. Describing it as 'the up-to-date LOWBRIDGE double-decker' may have conjured up visions of awkward side gangways in the minds of potential customers.

*Below:* This side elevation of a 1960 Dennis Loline II/East Lancs for North Western shows the low overall build and the flat platform with sliding door.

*Bottom:* The Dennis Loline was built between 1958 and 1966 and the last deliveries were five Loline III to Halifax with Northern Counties bodies. These had short lives there and were soon sold to West Riding to help out following its problems with the Guy Wulfrunian.

the up-to-date **LOWBRIDGE** "double-decker"

The Dennis LOLINE Double Deck Bus Chassis is an outstanding achievement of up to date design and engineering, giving a combination of the height of a low bridge double decker with the operational convenience of a normal height vehicle, it has too, central gangways in both upper and lower saloons allowing for speedier flow of passengers. Unusual features of the design contribute to the saving in height, an exceptionally low slung chassis having a transmission line offset so as to offer a much lower than usual central gangway in the lower saloon and the dispensation of the step between the rear platform and saloon. A unique design of the rear axle with a down arched central beam gives the necessary clearance for the low level gangway.
Powered by a Gardner 6LW Oil Engine and fitted with a Dennis five-speed gearbox, its ability to operate at low cost and increased passenger comfort, the Dennis Loline is indeed the up to date trend in double deck design.
An illustrated brochure giving full details will be sent free on request.

*low running costs*
*absolute reliability*
*remarkably manoeuvrable*

**DENNIS LOLINE P.S.V. CHASSIS**
DENNIS BROS LTD
GUILDFORD    SURREY

*Above:* AEC's last-ditch attempt at the lowheight market was the 1962 Renown, a separate chassis unlike the Bridgemaster, and a well-regarded bus that came just too late to win orders from operators who were considering the now-available rear-engined chassis. This is a 1963 delivery to South Wales Transport, with Park Royal body.

*Below:* Leigh Corporation needed lowheight double-deckers and bought 18 East Lancs-bodied Renowns between 1963 and 1967. This is from the first, 1963, batch. Metro-Cammell, Northern Counties, Park Royal, Roe, Weymann and Willowbrook all built bodywork for Renowns. The advert, right, shows one of the 1962 prototypes. *C. B. Golding*

RENOWN

From a line of buses of great renown comes the new Renown... the A.E.C. Renown for low height bodies of conventional construction. Here is a bus specifically designed by the world's leading bus specialists to give the widest utilisation and adaptability. A bus which can work both the low bridge routes and normal services. A bus offering probably the highest degree ever achieved in passenger comfort with orthodox seating. From its forward entrance to its rear air suspension, the Renown bristles with superior design features. Powered by the famous A.E.C. AV590 engine, and with alternative transmissions — "Monocontrol" or Synchromesh. Designed and manufactured by A.E.C.

A.E.C. LIMITED
SOUTHALL · MIDDLESEX

# United We Fall

In theory it makes sense to amalgamate several smaller players to create a larger, stronger company. That was the theory behind the spectacular growth of Leyland in the 1960s and the creation of United Bus in the late 1980s.

Two Dutch companies, DAF and Bova, were behind United Bus, which brought together DAF's bus interests with Bova, which manufactured integral coaches. DAF's trucks were not involved, but the main DAF company had a major stake in the new company.

The next move was an interesting one. Optare, the British company that had been set up in 1985 to produce

bus bodies in Leyland's former Roe factory in Leeds, joined United Bus in 1990. Optare had worked with DAF on the single-deck Delta and would work together on the Spectra double-decker. The same year United Bus took a 40 per cent share in DAB Silkeborg, Leyland's former Danish subsidiary, followed by Dutch bodybuilder Den Oudsten. In 1992 the Swiss bodybuilder, Ramseir & Jenzer was added to the group when a 50 per cent share in the business was bought.

In retrospect it was not a good time to be creating larger units as the bus and coach business was going through a tough patch, with operators cutting back on orders for new vehicles. But in spite of that, United Bus seemed to be little more than a loose amalgamation of companies that were allowed to carry on doing their own thing. Any

Before it joined United Bus, Optare already had a working relationship with DAF, which had led to the very stylish 1988-introduced Delta model, here for OK, Bishop Auckland.

thoughts that the companies in the group would benefit from economies of scale and exchange of ideas were quickly dispelled.

So it was no great surprise when in October 1993 United Bus collapsed – barely four years after it had been set up. DAB and Ramseir & Jenzer each reverted to wholly local ownership. Bova was sold to a group headed by its previous owners. DAF Bus was sold to the Dutch VDL Group. Den Oudsten struggled on but was declared bankrupt in 2002. And Optare was the subject of a management/employee buyout.

That wasn't the end of Optare's adventures. In the year 2000 it was bought by the Hungarian firm North American Bus Industries, but when NABI got into financial difficulties in 2005 Optare was bought back by its management. Then in 2008 it sold out to Jamesstan Investments, which also owned the East Lancs coachbuilding business and in a reverse takeover a new Optare company emerged, incorporating the East Lancs business.

So in spite of its ups and downs Optare survives and has built up an enviable reputation for stylish design and innovative engineering.

---

**OPTARE'S OWNERS**

| | |
|---|---|
| 1985 | Set up in former Roe factory |
| 1990 | United Bus |
| 1993 | Management/employee buyout |
| 2000 | NABI |
| 2005 | Management |
| 2008 | Jamesstan and new Optare Group |

*Left:* Optare was moving to become a manufacturer of complete vehicles and in 1989 had bought the rights to MCW's designs, including the MetroRider. This Cambus example was delivered during the United Bus period.

*Below:* In 1990, the year it joined United Bus, Optare introduced the Vecta midibus, based on MAN 11.190 chassis, as seen here for Black Prince, Morley.

# Bought Out or Sold Out?

Over half a century Leyland evolved into a solid, successful bus and truck builder with a range of bus chassis, engines and even complete vehicles that stood comparison with the best in the world. It had grown organically, with the odd acquisition, like Albion in 1951 and Scammell in 1955, and could well still be around today

The Leyland Tiger, introduced to compete with the Volvo B10M, was an important bus for Leyland in its final independent years. This is a Tiger prototype with Van Hool coach bodywork.

had it not embarked on an expansionist policy in the 1960s that, while perhaps not a bad thing in itself, dragged the company into the murky world of politics and the once-proud Leyland name became a national joke.

The 1960s expansion started with the Standard-Triumph car company in 1961 followed by arch-rivals AEC in 1962, creating the Leyland Motor Corporation, and AEC brought with it bodybuilders Park Royal and Roe. The AEC acquisition was at least in an area that Leyland understood. Mass-produced cars were something completely new.

The Olympian would prove to be hugely successful for Leyland and, after tweaking, for Volvo, and would survive to be the last Leyland-derived model on the bus market. Many earlier Olympians had ECW lowheight bodies like this Midland Red North example.

In 1965 a share exchange was engineered between Leyland and the Transport Holding Company, controlling the state-owned bus fleets as well as Bristol and ECW. Leyland acquired 25 per cent of Bristol and ECW, and THC got 29 per cent of Park Royal/Roe. The most obvious effect of this was to bring Bristol and ECW products back on to the open market again.

If the Standard-Triumph purchase caused Leyland problems, these were compounded in 1967 when it bought Rover. Things became even more difficult when Prime Minister Harold Wilson convinced Leyland to take on the ailing British Motor Holdings – the company formed when Jaguar merged with the British Motor Corporation in 1966. Jaguar had already acquired Daimler and Guy, so within the newly titled British Leyland Motor Corporation were Leyland and all of its serious rivals in the bus chassis business – AEC, Bristol, Daimler and Guy.

Some date the start of Leyland's downfall to the 1961 Standard-Triumph acquisition, and others to the creation of BLMC in 1968, but it would become very clear that here was a monster that could quickly get out of control. And of course it did.

Much BLMC management time was spent on the dying car business and so much money was being pumped in to save it that others parts of Leyland, which had been profitable, successful businesses, could only look on and weep.

Leyland's normally sure touch seemed to desert it. It rushed into a partnership with National Bus Company to develop and build the Leyland National citybus – a vehicle that nobody really wanted or needed at the time. It allowed London requirements to dictate what the rest of the country would get in its new-generation B15 double-deck, designed to replace the ageing Atlantean and

Fleetline. Operators, who seemed to have little choice but to buy BLMC models, rebelled by encouraging newcomers into the market, giving MCW, Scania and Volvo a foothold in the UK.

In short, Leyland lost its way on the bus front and operators grew tired of its arrogance and 'we know best' attitude.

British Leyland's problems continued through the 1970s into the 1980s, though it should be said that on the bus side things were looking more hopeful with successful models like the Olympian and Tiger. But BLMC was still causing headaches for the government, now Conservative and led by Margaret Thatcher, and in 1986 the company was being hawked round potential buyers. There was interest from various parties – Ford and Volkswagen were interested in the cars, General Motors in the trucks. What had become Leyland Bus attracted interest from an American entrepreneur and, interestingly, Laird Group, parent of MCW. In the early 1980s MCW had moved from being a bus bodybuilder to a builder of complete buses, with some success, and now it was a serious competitor. MCW's interest prompted Leyland to consider a management buyout and this led to the sale of Leyland Bus to a consortium of management and banks in January 1987.

Leyland's new owners were rewarded by orders from UK operators who were keen to support the new venture and happy to see ownership of Leyland stay in the UK. These same operators were far from happy when just 14 months later, in March 1988, it was announced that Leyland Bus had sold out to Volvo Bus. Although Volvo was a popular and trusted name in the UK bus market by this time, there was a feeling that their trust had been betrayed.

The Leyland name survived into the 1990s when the last Leyland Olympians entered service; the Olympian was the

*Right:* Leyland dipped its toe in the midibus market with two 9.5m buses from its Danish DAB factory in 1984. These were dubbed Tiger Cubs, but no more were built for the UK.

*Below:* The first Tiger Cub 'heavy-duty midibus' was built by DAB, but the second, seen here, was completed by ECW at Lowestoft and used by United Auto between 1985 and 1992.

one Leyland model still built by Volvo, and even that got the Volvo treatment in 1993 to emerge as the Volvo Olympian, which in fairness is regarded by many as the ultimate step-entrance double-decker.

It is interesting to speculate whether Leyland would have survived if it had steered clear of Harold Wilson's political wiles and avoided so much involvement in the mass car market.

If Lord Stokes had said no to Wilson, the proud Leyland name would not have become an object of ridicule and the company might have paid more attention to its product range and its customers. A more focused Leyland might have ridden out the storms of the 1980s to survive, probably in a very slimmed-down form. Doug Jack, in his book *Beyond Reality*, places the blame firmly at Margaret Thatcher's door. 'Even mighty international

corporations cannot live in hope,' he wrote. 'Nor can they predict phenomena like Margaret Thatcher and her wilful neglect of the country's manufacturing base. No other country which considers itself to be an important industrial nation would have done the damage she did.' He continued: 'Margaret Thatcher might have kept two thousand people in the Falklands, but she lost four million people in manufacturing industry in the United Kingdom during her premiership.'

Volvo inevitably dropped Leyland's models one by one, though it did recognise the value of the Olympian and went on to improve it further. Inevitably, too, it withdrew from production in the UK, although the Olympian continued to be built at the Irvine plant in Scotland. The last Volvo Olympian, arguably the last link with Leyland, was delivered in 2000 following more than 10,000 Olympian sales in a 20-year production run, more than half of these being Volvos.

In a way Dennis stepped into the Leyland breach, continuing the long tradition of UK-built chassis tailored specifically for the home market, and grew hugely in importance in the decade after Volvo acquired Leyland.

It is also interesting to speculate what would have happened if MCW had been able to buy Leyland and how this would have worked. Would MCW have developed its Metrobus at the expense of the Olympian? Would Leyland's Tiger have been developed into a serious alternative to Volvo's market-leading B10M? Would MCW's aborted lightweight bus of 1988 have given the Dennis Dart a run for its money? We do know that without Leyland in the fold, the Laird Group quickly closed down its bus-building activities.

Many UK operators were surprisingly loyal to Leyland through its BLMC period – sometimes, admittedly they had no real choice – and so felt betrayed when the management team, who had seemed determined to keep the business in UK control, sold out to Volvo.

## SIGNIFICANT LEYLAND DATES

| | |
|---|---|
| 1896 | Lancashire Steam Motor Company formed at Leyland, Lancashire |
| 1907 | Name changed to Leyland Motors Ltd |
| 1925 | Lion PLSC range introduced |
| 1927 | Tiger TS1 and Titan TD1 ranges introduced |
| 1949 | Leyland-MCW Olympic announced |
| 1951 | Albion acquired |
| 1956 | Atlantean prototype shown |
| 1959 | Leopard introduced |
| 1962 | ACV acquired |
| 1963 | Leyland Motor Corporation formed |
| 1965 | 25 per cent stake in Bristol and ECW acquired |
| 1968 | Merges with British Motor Holdings to form British Leyland Motor Corporation |
| 1970 | Leyland National introduced |
| 1977 | BL Truck & Bus Division becomes Leyland Vehicles Ltd |
| 1975 | British Leyland nationalised |
| 1980 | Olympian introduced |
| 1981 | Leyland Bus created |
| 1981 | Tiger launch |
| 1987 | Leyland Bus sold to management/banks consortium |
| 1988 | Volvo Bus acquires Leyland Bus |
| 1993 | Last 'Leyland' bus |

The Swift was another Leyland attempt to break into the small bus market, and was introduced following the Leyland Bus management buyout. It used Leyland DAF truck units, and this Hedingham & District delivery has Wadham Stringer Vanguard bodywork.

# Blunders in Brief

*Right:* The idea of a chassis that could be used as a basis for both single-deck and double-deck buses has been around for a while, and in truth there was often little mechanical difference between, say, an AEC Regal or Regent, or a Leyland Tiger or Titan. With underfloor-engined single-deckers the situation changed, but with the advent of rear-engined double-deckers the situation changed again. Great Yarmouth and Birkenhead corporations ordered Leyland Atlanteans with single-deck bodies, and single-deck bodies were built on Daimler Fleetlines and Dennis Dominators; the Fleetline SRG6 became a listed single-deck model. This Leyland Atlantean PDR2/1 with 40-seat Northern Counties body was ordered by Birkenhead Corporation but delivered to Merseyside PTE in 1970. Read more on this on pages 143/147.
*Michael Bennett*

*Right:* Atkinson was primarily a truck manufacturer that dabbled briefly in buses. Most were Gardner-engined single-deckers that found homes with a small group of faithful customers, but there was one PD746, this bus with centre-entrance Northern Counties body, delivered to the SHMD Board in 1955.

*Above:* The Dennis Falcon V coach was quickly put together for National Bus Company's Rapide coach services, with a view to this being a new premium British coach that would rival the imports from mainland Europe. Ten were built in 1982/83 with Duple Super Goldliner 47-seat high-floor bodies, but the rush to get these coaches on the road meant that they were not fully proved and they turned out to be less than reliable. This is a Western National example. The Falcon V featured a Perkins V8 engine; the Gardner-engined Falcon H did rather better as a bus chassis.

*Below left and below:* With Daimler Fleetline production scheduled to finish as British Leyland rationalised its double-deck range, other manufacturers saw this as an opportunity. Dennis fared rather well with its Dominator, but the Foden-Northern Counties barely got beyond prototype stage. Foden had dabbled in buses in the 1940s and 1950s and had built up an excellent reputation as a truck builder, but its rear-engined double-deck never took off. Seven were delivered, mainly to PTE fleets, but this was the example delivered to NBC's Potteries fleet in 1978.

*Right:* Dennis also tried its Falcon V model on the double-deck market, but with mixed success. Only six were built: 2 for Nottingham, 3 for Greater Manchester PTE; the sixth was the prototype. This is one of the two delivered to Nottingham in 1982. It has an East Lancs 88-seat two-door body to Nottingham's quirky style.

*Right:* British Coachways was a brave attempt to take advantage of the deregulation of express coach services in 1980 and compete with the might of National Express. It was an association of leading coach-operating companies – Grey-Green, Ellerman-Beeline, Park's of Hamilton, Shearings and Wallace Arnold. The coaches wore a patriotic red/white/blue livery, but this wasn't enough to keep it going. It is not easy trying to mould proud companies with very different cultures into a single entity and amid rumours of strong disagreements, first Grey-Green pulled out in 1981 and British Coachways simply disintegrated. This is a Grey-Green Leyland Leopard/Duple Dominant 2.

*Bottom:* British Coachways' publicity for its new services from Edinburgh in December 1980.

**New low-cost Express Coach Services from Edinburgh**

BRITISH COACHWAYS WHO INTRODUCED LOW COST EXPRESS COACH SERVICES TO BRITAIN IN OCTOBER ANNOUNCE EXTENDED SERVICES & NOW OPERATE DAILY TO. . .

**LONDON £8.50*** **NEWCASTLE £2.50**
**MIDDLESBRO' £3.00** **SUNDERLAND £2.50**
**LEEDS £4.50** **SHEFFIELD £5.00**

FARES SHOWN ARE SINGLE - SATURDAYS - ADD £1.00 ★LONDON ADD £2.50

DEPARTURE POINT: FREDERICK ST. EDINBURGH

BOOK NOW at
ELLERMAN TRAVEL, Frederick Street
Tel: 031-226-6911
or ANY TRAVEL AGENT

**British coachways** 🏴

see over for Full Schedules

# A London Non-Starter

The 1980 Transport Act that deregulated express coach services also opened the door to competition by making is easier for operators to compete with undertakings like London Transport, and while the most obvious outcome was the development of commuter coach services, there was a very real threat that the capital would be swamped with privately run minibuses.

In 1982 Associated Minibus Operators Ltd, AMOS, applied to operate up to 500 minibuses on high-frequency routes across London. There would be routes linking Wanstead to Crystal Palace, Muswell Hill to Sydenham, Richmond to Ilford, and Harlesden to Plumstead. The minibuses would be leased out to AMOS 'associates' who would operate them as well as garaging and maintaining them.

London Transport was also the licensing authority and it set up a public inquiry to look into the AMOS proposals. There were objections from London boroughs and, not unexpectedly, from London Transport and the taxi drivers' association.

LT's objections related to the effect the AMOS scheme would have on integration and the extra congestion it would bring to the roads. AMOS countered that it expected to take traffic from bus and underground services, taxis and minicabs and private cars. Under cross-examination, Anthony Shephard, AMOS's technical director, appeared to be shaky on some of the figures and forecasts he had provided, and his case was shot down by the report of the independent inspector, who criticised many of the firm's proposals.

The AMOS application was refused, but the company appealed and the appeal was heard in front of a Department of Transport inspector late in 1983. Although Shephard's figures had been rubbished first time round, Shephard

stuck with these and appeared to have learned little from the earlier hearing. LT then criticised many aspects of the scheme, suggesting that the minibuses would increase congestion and lead to higher fares, threaten integration and could spark service withdrawals.

The inspector's view that AMOS was 'not a reliable organisation to whom should be entrusted the introduction of a new private operation which could set an important precedent for the future' sealed the company's fate with the Transport Secretary, but recognised that minibuses in some form could have a part to play in London.

And of course that would be the case a short while later, but this time they were London Transport's minibuses and they would be used to develop routes with the intention of moving to larger buses as passenger numbers increased.

AMOS was a brave idea, prompted by the success of urban minibus systems overseas, often in Third World countries. In the spirit of the new freedoms encouraged by the Thatcher government, the scheme could have worked if it had been thought through and the company had done its sums properly. But in many ways it came as close as anything else to Nicholas Ridley's naïve and idealistic vision for privatisation with every bus in the control of its own owner-driver.

Although the AMOS scheme never got off the ground, London Transport did dabble with minibuses in the 1970s and increasingly in the 1980s. This is a 1985 Ford Transit/Carlyle 20-seater. *Keith Wood*

# Fair Fares Please

For some 30 years London Transport was allowed to go its own way with the minimum of political interference. From its creation in 1933, LT showed how a successful big city transport system should be run and though in retrospect some of its actions can be questioned, it worked and, importantly, its finances stayed in the black.

Since 1948 ultimate control of LT had rested with the state operating through the British Transport Commission, whose main preoccupation was the inherited and sprawling mainline railway network. BTC was abolished and in 1963 the London Transport Executive became the London Transport Board, responsible to the Minister of Transport.

The Greater London Council was created in 1964, initially with no responsibility for London Transport, but that changed at the start of 1970, paving the way for a series of clashes between the GLC and the Westminster government, and this was when political interference started creeping into the way London's transport was run.

In the 1960s and 1970s LT fares had on a couple of occasions been frozen at the government's 'request', but staff and fuel costs were rising fast and so the freezes were followed by above-average increases. In 1980 fares were increased twice, and when Labour won control of the GLC the following year Ken Livingstone became Leader of the Council. He went on of course to become the first Mayor of London, but from 1981 London politics under his control veered sharply to the left.

The GLC Labour group had promised a 25 per cent cut in fares in its manifesto, and Livingstone quickly took steps to initiate reductions that averaged 32 per cent: the 'Fares Fair' programme. The reductions were introduced in October 1981, bringing fares back to 1969 levels and resulting in a significant increase in passenger numbers.

But of course the money to recompense London Transport for the reduced income had to come from somewhere and it fell to London's ratepayers to fund the difference. The London Boroughs argued that Fares Fair was actually unfair as it subsidised people from beyond the GLC area who commuted into or visited London.

The London Borough of Bromley challenged the GLC's right to order such a big cut in fares, primarily because it was one of several boroughs not actually served by the tube that were being asked to subsidise tube fares. British Rail, which served Bromley, had declined to let the GLC subsidise its fares. Although the Divisional Court found in the GLC's favour, Bromley took the case to the Court of Appeal and the judgment was reversed. The GLC reluctantly accepted the call for the fares cut to be reversed and in March 1982 implemented a massive increase that averaged 96 per cent. Passenger numbers fell again, but the whole fiasco had highlighted the need for better subsidy arrangements and a simpler fares scale. So when fares were cut by 25 per cent in May 1983, fare zones were simplified and, most significantly, Travelcards were introduced that sensibly covered both bus and Underground services, and fares ended up pretty well where they had been when Livingstone first became involved.

One observer has suggested that if Livingstone had simply announced a fares freeze when he came into office, this would probably have gone unchallenged and the public would have enjoyed the benefits of a substantial saving in the real price of travel in London – and of course it would have avoided all the legal wrangles and the wide vacillations in the fares paid by the poor passengers.

If there is gain from the pain of Fares Fair, it is the belated appearance of the Travelcard and the simple fares that today's bus passengers pay in London.

# Through a Glass Darkly

It all really started in 1969 when London Transport Routemaster RM1737 appeared in an all-over advertising livery promoting Silexine paints. We thought – maybe hoped – that this form of advert would be a nine-day wonder, but the idea soon spread throughout the UK and spawned variations – back-end adverts, offside-only adverts and then contravision.

We understand that bus operators need to earn money in any way they can, although it is interesting to note that some of the best-regarded operators in the UK have renounced external advertising and the revenue it brings in, arguing that if such space is so attractive to advertisers, then bus companies should use it to promote their own wares.

Then someone came along with contravision, a film that can be applied over bus windows to allow advertisers (and operators, it must be said) to continue liveries over the widows. On a drawing-board or computer screen it probably looks fine with liveries that are not broken up by these nasty window things, but they steadily got worse to the stage where whole buses were covered in vinyls, and there were probably some agencies that would gladly have covered the driver's windscreen as well.

The odd swoop and swirl can probably be tolerated, but whole windows – no! Fare-paying passengers are doomed to watch the world through a fine black mesh that dulls the interior of the bus and makes identification of bus stops difficult, particularly at night.

You will have gathered that we don't really approve.

Vinyls on windows can give passengers an unsatisfactory view of their surroundings.

*Right:* A Reading Scania/ Wright with its side windows entirely covered by vinyls that tie in with its GreenPark FastTrack branding.

*Below:* The first overall painted advertising bus, London Transport Routemaster RM1737 in its Silexine livery.

# Seeing the Wood for the Trees

By the late 1980s the great vision for London Transport, created in 1933 to bring London's street and underground transport under one all-powerful body, was beginning to fade. Gone were the days of designing bespoke buses and buying them by the thousand, and disappearing quickly was a massive umbrella organisation with one address – the legendary 55 Broadway. National Bus Company was being broken up and privatised, and Scottish Bus Group and the PTEs would follow, so why not London Transport?

The 1933 London Passenger Transport Board became the London Transport Executive in 1948 in state ownership under the British Transport Commission, then in 1963 it became the London Transport Board reporting directly to the Minister of Transport. In 1970 it passed into the control of the new Greater London Council, then in 1980 to a new body, London Regional Transport, which created an arm's-length holding company, London Buses, to prepare for privatisation of the bus operations. Tendering of London bus services began in 1985 and several 'outside' companies were successful in winning tenders.

In 1988 London Buses created 11 new operating subsidiaries – CentreWest, East London, Leaside Buses,

Twilight for London Forest? A Leyland Titan TN15 in 1989 on night bus duties. *R. J. Waterhouse*

London Central, London Forest, London General, London Northern, London United, Metroline, Selkent, and South London. These ranged in size from Metroline (343 buses) to London General (582 buses) and they immediately stamped their individuality with the different types of bus they chose. Long gone were the days of the RT and Routemaster standardisation.

The companies now had to compete for London Transport tenders, but one of the 11 companies would quickly fall by the wayside.

In 1991 London Forest, which had started life with 361 buses, and garages at Ash Grove, Clapton, Leyton and Walthamstow, won the tenders for Walthamstow routes on the basis of reduced wage rates for existing employees. The only problem was that the company hadn't told the employees. For their part the employees were less than impressed and started a series of stoppages that escalated into an all-out strike. London Transport withdrew the tenders from London Forest and awarded them to County Bus & Coach, Capital Citybus and Thamesway. This prompted an announcement that Walthamstow garage would close, but very soon it was the London Forest company that had to close. Ash Grove garage also closed, with its work divided between East London, Leaside Buses and London Central. Leyton and Clapton garages were transferred to East London and Leaside Buses respectively.

The other 10 London Buses units survived and found new owners in 1994. Two (East London, Selkent) went to Stagecoach, which would later sell them on to Macquarie Bank; one (Leaside) went to Cowie, now Arriva; one (London Central) went to Go-Ahead; and one (London Northern) to MTL, which would later pass to Metroline. There were management/employee buyouts for the rest, though CentreWest went later to First, London General to Go-Ahead, London United to Transdev, Metroline to ComfortDelGro and South London to Cowie.

## LONDON FOREST TIMELINE

1988    London Forest subsidiary set up
1991    London Forest closed down

*Above:* Leyland Titan TN15s dominated the short-lived London Forest fleet and this one, displaying the London Forest logo above the entrance door, is at Walthamstow in 1988. *R. J. Waterhouse*

# The Sinking of Mayflower

One of the unhappiest and potentially most damaging episodes in the recent history of the UK's bus builders started when the Mayflower Corporation sailed into the bus industry. The Mayflower automotive group was involved in the design, engineering and manufacture of bodies for cars, light trucks and sports utility vehicles as well as commercial vehicle cabs, so an extension into bus and coach bodies and chassis probably seemed a logical one. Thus in 1995 it bought the Walter Alexander coachbuilding business, with factories in Scotland and Northern Ireland.

The Mini Pointer Dart was a staple TransBus product during the TransBus years; this MPD for Avondale carries no TransBus badging. *Gavin Booth*

That same year, Henlys, which owned Scarborough-based coachbuilder Plaxton, bought Northern Counties, the Wigan-based bus bodybuilder. Plaxton was enjoying success as a bus builder with its Pointer body for Dennis Dart chassis, and under Plaxton Northern Counties would go on to produce the successful President body for low-floor double-deckers.

Dennis, owned by Trinity Holdings, and Plaxton, owned by Henlys, had formed close links when they were developing the low-floor Dart SLF model and in 1998 announced that the two companies were merging, which on the face of it seemed like a logical move that would strengthen their presence in home and export markets.

The idea didn't appeal to Mayflower, who came in with

The Pointer range was built by TransBus at Falkirk, in the Alexander plant there. This is a Lothian SPD delivery.
*Gavin Booth*

a hostile bid for the Dennis business, which was successful. This left Plaxton out in the cold, with its major supplier of bus chassis now owned by a rival bodybuilder.

Although Plaxton started to hedge its bets by developing an integral midibus, two years later its problems were theoretically solved when its owners, Henlys, merged with Mayflower to create TransBus International.

A few years previously it would have seemed fanciful that the most significant force in the UK bus and coach building industry would be a company formed out of Alexander, Dennis and Plaxton, yet with TransBus International that is exactly what happened.

The new company faced immediate problems – too much bodybuilding production capacity (it had factories at Anston, Belfast, Falkirk, Scarborough and Wigan) and duplication in the model ranges. Although TransBus denied it, something would have to give.

To widespread disbelief it announced that the Plaxton plant at Scarborough would be closed, with the Pointer built at Falkirk and the coach bodies built elsewhere – possibly overseas. In the event, the Pointer transfer happened, but a slimmed-down Scarborough operation continued.

In 2003 TransBus launched the new Enviro200 model for its Falkirk-built bus range, but all was not well at Mayflower, which collapsed in 2004 and went into administration with a £20 million 'black hole' in the company's finances that threatened pension rights for staff.

The Scarborough coach business was the subject of a management buyout and the Plaxton name was quickly revived. The rest of TransBus, the Belfast, Falkirk, Guildford and Wigan plants, proved to be more of a problem and although there were rumours of overseas buyers moving in, a team of Scottish-based investors, including Stagecoach chairman Brian Souter in his personal capacity, mounted a rescue package and created Alexander Dennis Ltd. The Belfast business was closed, and the Wigan plant lasted only until 2005, but with much goodwill from customers Alexander Dennis rose from the ashes of Mayflower and TransBus and re-established its well-known brands. It even acquired Plaxton in 2007, reuniting the TransBus partners, but in a more financially stable business.

## MAYFLOWER – BEFORE AND AFTER

| | |
|---|---|
| 1989 | Plaxton buys Henlys |
| 1992 | Plaxton Group restructured as Henlys Group |
| 1995 | Henlys buys Northern Counties |
| | Mayflower buys Walter Alexander |
| 1998 | Henlys unsuccessfully bids for Dennis |
| | Mayflower buys Dennis |
| 2000 | Plaxton joint venture with Mayflower forms TransBus International |
| 2004 | Mayflower fails, TransBus into receivership |
| 2004 | Management buyout of Plaxton Consortium forms Alexander Dennis Ltd |
| 2005 | Alexander Dennis Wigan plant closes |
| 2007 | Alexander Dennis buys Plaxton |

*Above:* The Enviro300 was developed by TransBus and introduced in 2001. This 2003 delivery for First Edinburgh is liveried for services to the Falkirk Wheel. It carries the oval TransBus badge below the front screen. *Gavin Booth*

*Left:* The Falkirk coachworks has carried Walter Alexander, TransBus and, now, Alexander Dennis names on its Glasgow Road frontage. *Gavin Booth*

# Executive Decisions

Passenger Transport Executives, PTEs, were children of the far-reaching Transport Act 1968 that created, among other things, the National Bus Company and New Bus Grants. The premise was a logical one, regarding Britain's main conurbations as significant regions rather than a loose network of adjoining municipalities. In each case there was to be a policy-making body, the Passenger Transport Authority (PTA), with the PTEs carrying out policies on their behalf. Previously separate municipal bus operators were swept into the new PTE bus operations and old liveries and names gave way to new names and logos.

The first four PTEs – West Midlands, Selnec, Merseyside and Tyneside – were established between October 1969 and January 1970, and their operating areas would change with boundary readjustments in 1974 following the reorganisation of local government in England and the setting up of metropolitan counties. Two new PTEs were set up at this time: South Yorkshire and West Yorkshire. The six English PTEs between them mopped up 33 municipal bus undertakings and the one Scottish PTE, Greater Glasgow created in 1973, accounted for another one.

The PTEs had wide-ranging powers over road and rail transport and had a responsibility to co-ordinate services with other bus operators, which usually meant National Bus Company subsidiaries, and this was achieved in a

GM Buses was split into North and South companies before sale to employee/management teams. This is a GM South Leyland Olympian/Northern Counties in a GMS Express blue/cream livery. *R. L. Wilson*

range of ways, sometimes by acquisition, sometimes by standard liveries or fleetnames, while in some cases there was no outward sign of change.

When the metropolitan counties in England were abolished in 1986 the PTAs came back into play, while in Scotland regionalisation led to the renaming of Greater Glasgow PTE as Strathclyde PTE in 1975.

The Transport Act 1985 forced PTAs to sell off their bus fleets, which they did with some reluctance, and that was when the fun started. This of course was the legislation that introduced local bus deregulation, so the PTAs (again reluctantly, one suspects) lost the power to regulate fares and timetables, something the PTEs have more recently fought to regain.

The first sales of PTE companies went fairly smoothly. The first to go was West Yorkshire PTE, by now trading as Yorkshire Rider, which was sold to its management and employees in 1988.

In 1986 what had been Tyne & Wear PTE's bus operations became Busways Travel Services and in 1989 this company was sold to its employees and management.

West Midlands Travel was also sold to its management and employees, in 1991, and although there had been moves before it was sold to break the company up into smaller units, it was sold as a single entity. Stagecoach had shown an interest in WMT, but was not allowed to bid.

In 1992 Merseyside Transport was sold out to its management and employees, followed by Strathclyde Buses in 1993, and Mainline (South Yorkshire), which went to its employees the same year.

So far, so good. Six down, and all to management-employee teams, a result that seemed to make good local political sense.

The remaining PTA, Greater Manchester, had very different ideas. It had told the government in 1990 that it didn't want to sell its bus operations, and the response was

*Above:* GM Buses North publicity, featuring new Volvo B10B/Wright buses. Although promoted as 'low floor', they were step-entrance buses.

*Below:* The South Yorkshire PTE bus operations became Mainline, which was a major customer for the Volvo B10M/Alexander PS type combination. *Lee M. Whitehead*

*Right:* Yorkshire Rider experimented with guided buses, which led to the East Leeds busway scheme. This is a Scania N113/ Alexander Strider on a short stretch of busway.

*Below:* Delivered to Yorkshire Rider during its management/employee-owned phase, a new Leyland Olympian/ Alexander RL type in 1990 at Bradford Interchange – itself a grand scheme that provided a massive road/rail interchange and bus garage, and which never realised its real potential. *Adrian A. Thomas*

a threat that the bus company would be split before being sold off. It was – into GM Buses North and GM Buses South – and late in 1993 preferred bidders were announced. South would go to its management/employee buyout team, while North would go to British Bus – Drawlane as was, the group that would metamorphose into Cowie then Arriva.

This was not good news for the North management/employee buyout team, who argued that this would give British Bus an even stronger presence in north-west England, where it already had sizeable operations on Merseyside and in and around Manchester.

Early in 1994 Greater Manchester PTA decided that it was not going to accept the British Bus offer but would accept the management/employee buyout bid. West Midlands Travel had made a bid for North and Stagecoach for South, but these were unsuccessful in spite of a Stagecoach promise to invest in 125 new single-deck buses for the area, and the PTA decision prompted Stagecoach to do a bit of sabre-rattling by creating Stagecoach Manchester, run by its Ribble subsidiary, running from the city centre south to Hazel Grove.

During the arms-length ownership period, two West Midlands Travel MCW Metrobuses in Coventry in 1987. *Kevin Lane*

The same year Stagecoach acquired a 20 per cent stake in Mainline, prompting the Monopolies & Mergers Commission, which had taken an almost obsessive interest in bus operations around Sheffield, to announce that it would investigate Stagecoach's shareholding. In 1995 the MMC forced Stagecoach to divest this shareholding, and the newly created FirstBus took it over.

Later in 1994 Stagecoach announced that it would compete in Glasgow with Strathclyde Buses, through its recently acquired Western Scottish company. Strathclyde retaliated with the threat of services in Stagecoach's hometown of Perth, but instead Stagecoach acquired a 20 per cent stake in Strathclyde's owners, SB Holdings. This shareholding also came under MMC scrutiny and it was concluded that the merger situation was against the public interest and recommended that Stagecoach should be required to divest itself of its shareholding in SBH.

Stagecoach eventually got what it wanted in Manchester when in 1996 it bought GM Buses South, having sold its previous Stagecoach Manchester operation to EYMS Group. The same year FirstBus bought GM Buses North.

These hadn't been the first sales of former PTE bus companies by their management and employees. With other strong and recently privatised companies

In Tyne & Wear, Busways split its operation into different areas with different colours added to the basic yellow and white. This former London Buses Leyland Olympian/Northern Counties is in the City Busways livery, with the words 'An Employee Owned Company' added to the fleetname. *Malcolm King*

surrounding it, Busways had decided to sell out to Stagecoach in 1994.

The others didn't take long to follow in selling out to the big groups: Rider Holdings (West Yorkshire) to Badgerline in 1994, West Midlands Travel to National Express in 1996, Strathclyde to First in 1996, Mainline (South Yorkshire) to First in 1998 and lastly Merseyside to Arriva in 2000.

So the big groups got what they wanted at the end of the day, but not before they had to go through the hoops when their offers were turned down or they were referred to the MMC.

A couple of the PTAs bounced back into street transport operation with the Manchester Metrolink and Sheffield Supertram projects, both now run by Stagecoach; and the PTE Group, PTEG, has been vocal in its call for re-regulation of bus services, or at least quality contracts where they will have more control over routes, services, fares and frequencies. The bus operators, not surprisingly, tended to disagree, but more than 40 years after their

initial creation the PTAs are showing that they are still a force to be reckoned with.

## PTE SALES

### First round

| | |
|---|---|
| 1988 | Yorkshire Rider to management/employees |
| 1989 | Busways to management/employees |
| 1991 | West Midlands Travel to management/employees |
| 1992 | Merseyside to management/employees |
| 1993 | Strathclyde to management/employees |
| 1993 | Mainline to employees |
| 1993 | GM Buses South to management/employees |
| 1994 | GM Buses North to management/employees |

### Second round

| | |
|---|---|
| 1994 | Busways to Stagecoach |
| 1994 | Rider to Badgerline |
| 1996 | GM Buses South to Stagecoach |
| 1996 | GM Buses South to First |
| 1996 | West Midlands Travel to National Express |
| 1996 | Strathclyde to First |
| 1998 | Mainline to First |
| 2000 | Merseyside to Arriva |

# Unpainted and Unwanted

Painting buses can be costly and time-consuming and in the 1950s several operators experimented with unpainted buses. Not painting buses, it was argued, would make economic sense and would also reduce the weight of the bus by up to 3cwt at a time when manufacturers and operators were agonising over this to cut fuel costs. In theory, accident damage on an unpainted bus could also be repaired more quickly.

Buying buses unpainted was said to save up to £90 – but this was at a time when new double-deckers cost around £4,500, so it was perceived as a worthwhile saving. As was the whole-life saving of around £300 per bus.

London Transport had introduced experimental unpainted Underground stock in 1952 and this was spread to become the Underground fleet standard. So a handful of British bus operators ordered buses with unpainted finishes. Some fleets, including London Transport, had just one unpainted bus, but others went for small batches to test the durability and public reaction. The best-known experiments were at Edinburgh, Liverpool and South Wales Transport, and while the buses looked OK when they were brand-new, some quickly lost their sheen and looked, frankly, dull and unattractive.

Buses with plain aluminium panels seemed to survive better than those with embossed panels. Edinburgh

One of Edinburgh Corporation's 11 unpainted buses – Leyland Titans with Metro-Cammell Orion bodies. They were painted in fleet colours within four years.

Corporation chose the Birmabright finish, using embossed panels that turned out to hold the dirt and quickly gave the bus a grey appearance. Edinburgh had to treat the panels with lanolin every six months, which cancelled out some of the cost savings.

Other problems with unpainted buses included the difficulty of applying transfers and sticking adverts to the bare panels.

Most operators had painted their unpainted buses within two or three years, but London Transport persevered with one Routemaster, RM664, which first appeared in 1961, after some operators had abandoned the idea, and ran at various garages until 1965 when it was taken in for painting in normal LT red.

Like other 'unpainted' buses, RM664 was not actually entirely unpainted; any external parts that were not aluminium, like the bonnet top, had to be painted silver to match the rest of the body.

*Above:* Liverpool Corporation stuck with its unpainted buses longer than most. This is a 1961 Leyland Titan PD2/30 with Crossley/Metro-Cammell bodywork to Liverpool specification. *John Robinson*

*Right:* In addition to its unpainted trains, London Transport operated a Routemaster in unpainted finish, RM664. *G. Mead*

*Above:* Later, for the Queen's Silver Jubilee in 1977, London Transport painted 25 of its Routemasters silver, and temporarily renumbered them SRM1-25. SRM16 here, sponsored by Kleenex, was really RM1920.
*G. Mead*

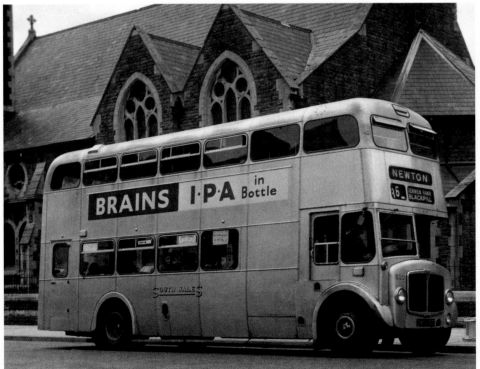

*Left:* South Wales Transport briefly favoured unpainted buses, like this 1959 AEC Regent V with Weymann forward entrance body.
*John H Napier*

# Leave Your Troubles Behind

Just where bus engines should be positioned has long exercised the minds of manufacturers. At first it seemed natural that the engine should be at the front, as in a motorcar, and for the first 40-odd years of the motorbus this was where it was usually found – first with the driver behind it and then with the driver perched up beside it. And that seemed to work fine.

The first and the best: a late-model (1973) Colchester Corporation Bristol RELL when new. The curved-screen ECW body on the low-built RELL chassis is widely regarded as an all-time classic. *Gavin Booth*

There have always been people who have been prepared to question accepted wisdom. Sometimes those were operators and sometimes manufacturers; sometimes even a combination of both.

In the 1930s London Transport had worked with Leyland to produce a flat-engined single-decker, the TF type, and a small rear-engined single-decker, the CR type. And AEC, which had enjoyed some success with its side-engined Q in the 1930s, was developing an underfloor-engined Regal. A prototype had been built for Canada in 1939 and the production Regal IV was launched a decade later.

Midland Red had ploughed its own furrow and its own-build BMMO bus designs included rear-engined prototypes that were transformed into underfloor-engined buses during World War II, allowing Midland Red to start production of its pioneering S6 type in 1946.

The successes and failures of the early underfloor-engined single-deckers are chronicled elsewhere in this book, but even as underfloor single-deckers were becoming universally accepted, manufacturers were looking at rear-mounted engines. Leyland had proved with its rear-engined Atlantean double-decker that this layout was practical and helped operators achieve maximum seating capacities. This was not a problem with single-deckers as tucking the engine away under the floor allowed a front-mounted entrance, ahead of the front wheels, and an open saloon with space for up to 45 passengers.

The problem perceived by some operators and manufacturers was the inevitable height of the floor. With a chunky engine and gearbox mounted amidships under the floor, that floor level had to be high, with several steps

to be negotiated from the roadside to the seats. A rear-engined single-decker could bring floor levels down, certainly at the entrance and in the front portion of the bus ahead of the rear axle.

Although several manufacturers seem to have had their 'eureka' moment around the same time, it was Bristol that managed to design a practical rear-engined model, the RE, in 1962. Bristol was able to test its prototypes with its customers, restricted to state-owned fleets, and iron out any bugs before going into series production. The RE with its front-mounted radiator and horizontal engine behind the rear axle – usually a chunky Gardner 6HLW or 6HLX – got it pretty well right first time. The trouble was nobody else quite managed to match the RE's reliability and sales success.

That didn't stop them trying, though.

Daimler, which was enjoying success with its Fleetline double-deck chassis, chose the 1962 Commercial Motor Show to launch its new rear-engined single-deck chassis. This featured a low frame, a step-free entrance and dropped front and rear axles to provide a flat floor over most of the length of the 36ft-long vehicle. The prototype SRD6 had a transversely-mounted 125bhp Daimler MkVIII 8.6-litre horizontal engine that could become a 150bhp unit with turbocharging. Contemporary publicity said that Gardner

In sales terms the AEC Swift family was quite successful – helped of course by all those London Transport orders. This is a Morecambe & Heysham 1970 Swift with Northern Counties 50-seat two-door body. *R. Johnson*

*Above:* Preston Corporation built up a sizeable fleet of Leyland Panthers between 1968 and 1972, including some second-hand examples. This is a 1971 Panther with Pennine bodywork. *Edward Shirras*

*Right:* Leyland's Panther was promoted heavily in the trade press. This 1967 advert shows the chassis, which shared much with the contemporary AEC Swift.

6HLW or 6HLX engines would be available, and it was perhaps a misjudgement to show it with a Daimler engine when most operators would have chosen a Gardner.

The Daimler chassis had great potential, but between the 1962 and 1964 Commercial Motor Shows Daimler had a change of heart and developed the Roadliner, with a Cummins V6-200 engine. Elsewhere in the book the sad story of the Roadliner is related along with photos showing the 1962 prototype and Roadliner chassis. In 1968 Daimler introduced a single-deck version of its Fleetline chassis, the SRG6, which proved to be marginally more successful than the unhappy Roadliner, though a very different type of chassis. It could be built alongside Fleetline double-deckers, and most of its customers already had double-deck Fleetlines in their fleets. Three of the operators that had bought Roadliners – Belfast, Darlington and Potteries – seemed prepare to forgive Daimler and chose single-deck Fleetlines.

Leyland clearly couldn't allow rival manufacturers to steal a march and the Leyland Motor Corporation, formed

The lighter and shorter Leyland Panther Cub was favoured by some operators, mainly in the municipal sector, though sales just failed to reach the 100 mark in four years of production. This is an Oldham Corporation example with Marshall 45-seat two-door body, one of four delivered in 1967.

following the 'merger' of AEC and Leyland in 1962, introduced two new chassis in 1964: the AEC Swift and Leyland Panther. These models shared a common chassis but with the AEC AH505 engine in the Swift (and the big AH691 in what would become known as the Merlin) and the Leyland O.600 in the Panther. These models took advantage of the relaxing of length regulations that allowed 36ft-long buses from 1961. Leyland also introduced a 33ft rear-engined chassis, the Panther Cub, with its O.400 engine, and shorter Swifts were also built.

In the end respectable sales were achieved for the AEC and Leyland models, with London Transport committing itself to a massive fleet of Swifts and Merlins that proved to be less than successful in service, as recounted elsewhere in this book.

One rear-engined chassis from Leyland that was rather different from its contemporaries was the Albion Viking VK43. This was not a sophisticated low-slung chassis aimed at city fleets but a simpler and more rugged model designed largely with Scottish Bus Group orders in mind. SBG was in the 1960s withdrawing 35-seat front-engined single-deckers and was looking for a low-cost vehicle for the more rural duties that these buses typically performed. SBG took

more than 200 Vikings between 1965 and 1969, and the model went on to be popular in export markets, particularly Australia. The Viking had the Leyland O.400 engine mounted vertically in-line at the rear, with a rear radiator.

Leyland's influence spread with the Bristol/ECW share exchange in 1965 and the creation of British Leyland in 1968 which brought Daimler into the fold. With AEC, Bristol, Daimler and Leyland rear-engined single-deckers on its lists, British Leyland was clearly going to do a bit of rationalising. It did this by designing a completely new bus with the new National Bus Company, the Leyland National, launched in 1970, and to recoup some of its investment and force operators to buy the National it withdrew its competing models. The Merlin/Swift, Panther/Panther Cub and Roadliner may not have been widely mourned, but the Bristol RE was selling better than ever. In 1971 it achieved its best-ever sales of 643 chassis, and had benefited from almost a decade of constant development. Following Leyland's stake in Bristol, the RE was being chosen by a widening group of customers beyond the state-owned sector, but Leyland wasn't going to let anything get in the way of National sales.

The last home-model RE chassis were built in 1975, but the RE enjoyed a resurgence as an export model, with sales to Christchurch, New Zealand (152 chassis) and to Citybus and Ulsterbus in Northern Ireland, who were counted as 'export' customers to give Leyland a continued foothold there, and who received 600 REs, the last in

1983, although the last only entered service in 1986. In total, 4,629 REs were built between 1962 and 1983.

Part of the rush to buy rear-engined single-deckers in the UK was caused by the regulations that only permitted driver-only operation of single-deckers and many operators were looking to make economies by dispensing with conductors. No sooner had the first round of rear-engined models appeared in the mid-1960s than driver-only double-deckers were permitted, in 1966, and many operators who had turned to single-deckers reverted to double-deckers.

With only the National available from Leyland, other manufacturers eyed the single-deck market and particularly noted the success of the Bristol RE. What was wanted, they concluded, was a Gardner-engined chassis, and first on the scene, even before the National was announced, was Seddon with its RU in 1969, but in spite of a couple of reasonable orders – notably 100 for NBC's Crosville fleet – only 272 were built.

Dennis had a go with its Falcon H, again Gardner-engined, but only 122 were sold in 13 years from 1981.

A potentially more serious rival for the Leyland National was the Metro-Scania, a collaboration between MCW and Scania. MCW could see that sales of single-deck bodies could be affected by the forthcoming Leyland National and came up with this sophisticated alternative, but barely

130 were built between 1969 and 1973, with the municipal fleets at Leicester and Newport as the principal customers. Leicester had also been a major customer for the Dennis Falcon H, reflecting its dissatisfaction with Leyland products.

Even Volvo had a go at this market, in 1972, with a B59 demonstrator fitted with a Marshall Camair body. Volvo was still a relative newcomer to the UK bus and coach market, and was enjoying some decent sales for its B58 underfloor-engined coach chassis, but the B59 was possibly too sophisticated for the UK, and too expensive, and the demonstrator remained unique.

## REAR-ENGINED SINGLE-DECK 1960s TIMELINE

| First built | | Last built |
|---|---|---|
| 1962 | Bristol RE | 1984 |
| | Daimler prototype | – |
| 1964 | AEC Merlin/Swift | 1975 |
| | Daimler Roadliner | 1972 |
| | Leyland Panther/Panther Cub | 1972 |
| 1965 | Albion Viking | 1969 |
| 1966 | Daimler Fleetline SRG6 | 1973 |
| 1969 | Seddon RU | 1974 |
| 1969 | Metro-Scania | 1973 |

The Albion Viking, with its vertical rear engine and constant-mesh gearbox, was clearly not designed for sophisticated city operation.

*Above:* An early Albion Viking/Alexander Y type delivery to Eastern Scottish for coach touring work, newly delivered in 1965. *Gavin Booth*

QUINAG FROM LOCH NEDD

SCOTLAND'S GLORY

SCOTLAND'S PRIDE

GLASGOW 8B

®ALB 3/6825

# Vikings attack RISING TRANSPORT COSTS

The Viking VK43AL, built by Albion on Clydeside, is the wise way of attacking transport costs. Like all Albion vehicles it is built to the exacting engineering standards which have made Scots famous throughout the world.

With rear-mounted vertical engine the Viking has plenty of front entrance space for one-man operation, excellent weight distribution for good tyre life and passenger comfort, easy access for servicing.

The chassis is designed for bus operation at 20 160 lb g.v.w. (43 seats) or for coach operation at 21 280 lb g.v.w. (41 seats).

Powered by the economical Leyland 400 diesel, it has an Albion 5 speed gearbox with optional overdrive 6th and of course—an Albion hub reduction rear axle.

Take a tip from a cost conscious operator and let Albion Vikings attack your fleet costs. Albions—*you can depend on them!*

BUILT IN SCOTLAND
FOR THE DISCERNING OPERATOR

BRITISH
LEYLAND

Albion

ALBION MOTORS LIMITED, SCOTSTOUN, GLASGOW W.4.   Telephone: Scotstoun 1261-70
OVERSEAS SALES: BERKELEY SQUARE HOUSE, BERKELEY SQUARE, LONDON, W.1. Telephone: 01-499 6060

*Left:* The Scottish roots of the Albion Viking VK43 are emphasised in this 1968 trade advert featuring an Alexander-bodied example for Alexander (Midland), part of the Scottish Bus Group and a target customer for the model.

*Above:* The Metro-Scania had the greatest potential to give the Leyland National some serious competition, but sales were poor. This is a 1970 delivery to London Country for its innovative SuperBus network in Stevenage, where Metro-Scanias worked alongside Leyland Nationals.

# listen to this

Some facts relating to vehicle noise and its reduction

THE QUIET BUS

# METRO·SCANIA
THE "SILENT" BUS  (noise level about 77 dB(A))  (Patents pending)

*Right:* MCW and Scania had early concerns about vehicle noise, though some of the scientific explanations inside this leaflet verge on the obvious. 'If you are standing alone at the roadside and a car is coming towards you, it is noticeable how the noise increases the closer the car comes.' Er, yes. Or 'The intensity of the noise decreases with the distance from the sound source.' Amazing!

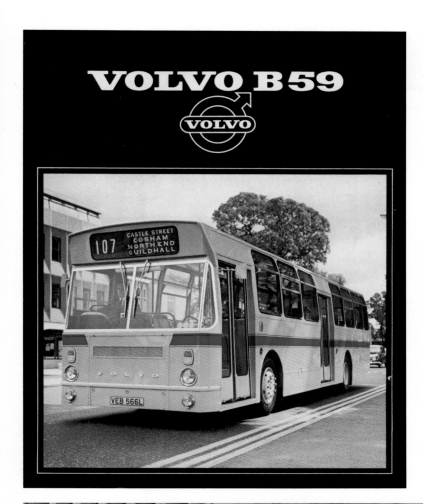

*Left:* Volvo, which was just starting to make an impact on the UK coach scene with its B58 chassis, also tested the water with the rear-engined B59 bus chassis.

*Below:* The bus shown on the Volvo brochure cover, with Marshall Camair body, would be the only one imported. It is seen here on demonstration in Liverpool.

*Above:* Although Dennis kept the Falcon H chassis on its lists for 13 years, sales reached only 122. Ipswich bought 19 between 1985 and 1989; this is a 1986 example with Northern Counties 44-seat body.

*Right:* Doncaster Corporation was an early customer for Seddon's RU and bought three batches between 1970 and 1974. Although most bodywork on RUs was built by Seddon's in-house Pennine team, a number were built by Plaxton, mainly for Lancashire United, and Lancashire municipalities favoured East Lancs, the only examples bodied by Roe were 11 of these Doncaster examples, new in 1972.

# One Size Fits All

For some manufacturers, the idea of a universal chassis that could carry both single-deck and double-deck bodies has been seen as something of a panacea. And you can understand why: for the manufacturers, no need to build a wide range of models; and for the operators, standardisation and fewer spare parts to stock.

It almost happened in the 1930s when models like AEC's Regal and Regent, or Leyland's Tiger and Titan, were not hugely different other than in length and wheelbase. When single-deck and double-deck buses became very different in the 1950s with the adoption of underfloor-engined single-deckers, any thoughts of standardisation had to be abandoned. And then of course double-deckers went to big rear-mounted engines, which attracted some operators to use double-deck chassis for single-deckers, but rear-engined single-deckers generally went for flat engines under the floor at the rear.

South Wales Transport found it necessary to specify double-deck chassis for its Llanelli Docks route because of low overhead clearances. In 1962 it bought six AEC Regent V chassis fitted with Roe 37-seat single-deck bodies.

A Bristol VRL/LH chassis – in fact one destined for Johannesburg – showing the layout with front-mounted radiator and in-line engine mounted at the rear offside, and clearly different from any existing rear-engined chassis on the market at the time. Although intended as a single-deck or double-deck chassis, the VRL was built only as a double-decker.

Daimler, perhaps reacting to the poor image of its Roadliner chassis, introduced a single-deck Fleetline and sold this very much on the basis of fleet standardisation, which appealed to some operators.

But other attempts were less successful.

Bristol, for instance, recognised the potential for a universal rear-engined chassis in the 1960s and development work started on what was known as the N type in true Bristol fashion. Prototype chassis to 33ft and 36ft lengths were produced, and these differed from other contemporary models with their low frame and longitudinally-mounted engine in the rear offside corner. Conceived as a single-deck or double-deck chassis, the N type, soon renamed VRL (Vertical Rear Longitudinal) was only bodied as a double-decker; the successful RE model was what operators looking for Bristol single-deckers were happy to choose.

The VRL was not a huge success as a double-decker either, with two prototypes, 30 coaches for Ribble/Standerwick, and 25 buses for South Africa – 14 for Johannesburg and 11 for Pretoria. The VR chassis was reworked as the VRT, with a transverse engine that brought it more into line with the Daimler Fleetline and Leyland Atlantean, and in this form sold nearly 4,500 examples.

Dennis went down the universal chassis route with the Falcon V model, which sold only 16 – 10 single-deck coaches and six double-deck buses. The Dennis Dominator double-deck chassis was chosen for 36 single-deckers delivered to various operators in 1978-80. Dennis returned briefly to the theme with the Arrow double-deck chassis, introduced in 1996 and based on the single-deck Lance with its in-line Cummins engine, but it was rather overtaken by the move to low-floor double-deckers and only 73 were built.

Volvo made several attempts to convince operators that the same chassis could be used as a basis for both single-deck and double-deck buses. The Ailsa was Volvo's main double-deck chassis, uniquely front-engined at the time, and one was bodied as a single-decker in 1983 for Strathclyde PTE.

Lacking a rear-engined double-deck chassis in the 1970s and early 1980s, Volvo developed the Citybus, which was essentially its successful mid-engined B10M chassis, with a perimeter frame for double-deck bodies; later Citybuses were virtually standard B10M chassis. It was the first underfloor-engined double-decker to go into production for the UK market and proved very successful, in spite of the essentially high floor level.

Inspired perhaps by this success Volvo introduced its new low-floor double-deck in 1999, based on its new B7L single-deck chassis. Operators who wanted the more familiar transversely-mounted engine and a short rear overhang were less than complimentary about the prototype, with its engine mounted in the rear nearside corner and long overhang, so Volvo rushed back to the drawing-board and conceived the B7TL to meet UK requirements. The B7L has since sold with double-deck bodywork, but principally as the basis of an open-topper, though First Glasgow did take 10 three-axle buses with East Lancs bodies, a type that was subsequently bought for use in Copenhagen.

In theory the universal bus makes a lot of sense, but UK operators still have very firm ideas about chassis layouts for single-deck and double-deck buses, although chassis components are increasingly common between both types.

*Above:* The Daimler Fleetline enjoyed some success as a single-deck chassis, usually with operators who also ran the double-deck version. This is a 1970 Belfast Corporation delivery with Alexander Belfast body.

*Left:* Grimsby-Cleethorpes Transport bought single-deck and double-deck Daimler Fleetlines, and this 1966 SRG6/Willowbrook was exhibited at the 1966 Commercial Motor Show when the model was introduced.

*Right:* Darlington Transport was the first operator to order a single-deck Dennis Dominator, and this was the first such bus built – a 1978 delivery with Marshall Camair 80 bodywork.

*Below:* The Dennis Falcon V chassis was sold in very restricted numbers as the basis of a luxury coach and a double-decker. Dennis claimed that the rear-mounted in-line vee engine would save weight and cost, giving increased seating capacity in a double-decker.

*Above:* The most successful single-deck/double-deck crossover was the Volvo Citybus, based on its best-selling B10M chassis. Although the high build necessitated by the mid-engine mounting could have been a problem – both for passengers and for tilting the bus successfully when new – the Citybus enjoyed decent sales success. This is the first one, built with Marshall body for Strathclyde PTE in 1982.

*Left:* The essentially high build of the Volvo Citybus did not hamper sales, which included batches to Derby City Transport, including ten in 1984 with a revised style of Marshall bodywork.

# Taken for Granted?

It seemed like a good idea at the time. As part of the huge upheavals in the UK bus industry caused by the 1968 Transport Act, the government was introducing a New Bus Grant to encourage the purchase of new buses suitable for driver-only operation. At the same time the Act was setting up the National Bus Company and Scottish Transport Group, and creating the first four Passenger Transport Executives, so there was a lot happening.

Never guilty of passing up a bargain, bus operators rushed to take advantage of Bus Grants.

The scheme was not totally open-ended, however. It specified the buses you could buy that would attract the grant – 25 per cent as originally conceived. Double-deckers had to be 9.5m lowheight or 9.5m or 10m normal height buses, and every dimension was (superfluously, perhaps) laid out in detail. On the 10m buses the exit had to be in the centre, the 9.5m normal height buses could have front or centre exits, and the 9.5m lowheight buses could only have front exits.

What were described officially as 'single-deck low-floor buses', though not low-floor in the present-day

The New Bus Grants scheme sounded the death-knell for long-running – and still popular – models like Leyland's Titan. Some operators continued to buy front-engined double-deckers as long as they could, even as here with a traditional exposed radiator rather than a full-width front. This is a 1969 delivery to Stockport Corporation, a Titan PD3 with East Lancs forward-entrance body; at the same time Stockport was buying similar buses with open rear entrances.

interpretation, had to be 10m or 11m rear underfloor-engined or transverse underfloor-engined buses, and in every case they could be one-door or two-door buses.

'Single-deck high-floor buses', essentially mid-engined buses, could be 9m, 10m or 11m long, but only with single front doors.

This took account of much of what was on the market at the time, though it sounded the death-knell for the remaining front-engined double-deckers – the last examples of long-running types like the AEC Regent and Routemaster, Bristol Lodekka, Daimler CVG6 and Leyland Titan entered service between 1968 and 1970. Most operators had moved on to rear-engined double-deckers by that time anyway, but there were still some engineers who hankered after the sturdy simplicity of a front-engined design.

Another consequence of the 1968 Act was that stand-alone often standardised fleets were now compromised by their new bedfellows. National Bus Company united the highly standardised Bristol/ECW-dominated Tilling Group with the rather more varied BET Group, so New Bus Grants provided an ideal opportunity to replace non-standard types with NBC's preferred types – increasingly the Leyland National and the Bristol VRT. For the new PTEs this was a chance to root out the oddball vehicles they had acquired and stamp their authority with large injections of new and standardised buses.

Faced with a highly varied selection of buses from the municipal fleets they inherited, the new PTEs set about creating standard designs that would be rolled out in their hundreds in the name of fleet standardisation. Selnec, in Greater Manchester, had a number of experimental buses built before finalising its choice, and this is EX4, a 1970 Leyland Atlantean with Northern Counties body that would be followed by over 1,200 broadly similar buses and 500 similar Fleetlines over the next 14 years – all bought with the aid of the (rapidly decreasing) grants. *C. B. Golding*

For other operators who had invested in single-deckers in the 1960s to increase driver-only operation this was a chance to rid themselves of unsuitable buses, often with barely a decade under their belts, in favour of new buses – often double-deckers now that these could be one-person operated.

There was a fairly unseemly scramble for new buses, particularly following the 1971 increase in the New Bus Grant to 50 per cent, but around the corner was a period of economic unease, fuel crises and the three-day week. New deliveries in 1974, for example, bore little relationship to the orders in hand as chassis parts dried up and the bodybuilders had to twiddle their thumbs until chassis started to arrive. In 1974 just under 5,000 buses were on order for local authorities, and already some of these were up to two years late. That year some 2,675 Daimler Fleetlines were on order, for example – roughly four years'

New Bus Grants encouraged operators to buy coach-like vehicles for lighter duties. This is a 1973 Potteries Ford R1114 with Duple Dominant Express 49-seat body operating on one of the company's more rural routes.

production, a situation aggravated by Leyland's decision to switch Fleetline production from Coventry to Leyland.

Leyland's monopoly further aggravated the situation as operators often had no choice than to buy from Leyland, which at that time also included AEC, Bristol and Daimler. Some competing models appeared in the early 1970s and this helped to take up the slack; the MCW/Scania Metropolitan and Volvo Ailsa appeared in 1973 and although they won orders – often protest orders from frustrated bus companies – they lacked the capacity to reduce the backlog of orders.

As the 1970s progressed, the situation eased and operators became more adept at playing the system, particularly if they could recoup half the cost of a new bus. Smaller operators that had previously relied on second-hand buses as well as coaches that doubled up on what was then known as stage carriage work found that they could qualify for the grant if they bought coaches that had a few simple tweaks – mainly the use of power-operated doors.

The use of 'grant coaches' spread to the larger operators as well, and the only discipline was to ensure that the majority of their work was on stage work rather than express services or tours, which obviously was a temptation.

At the time the New Bus Grants scheme seemed like a good idea, but on reflection it distorted the economics of bus operation, encouraging some operators to scrap perfectly good 10-year-old buses rather than keep them longer as before. And as it inflated the market artificially, too much capacity was chasing an unrealistic assessment of demand, leading to the collapse of the manufacturing industry in the 1980s when the grant was phased out. It also fed inflation in the price of new buses. It is tempting to wonder if bus manufacturers pushed prices up in the knowledge that operators looking for a 50 per cent rebate were unlikely to complain.

And manufacturers had to move quickly because the 50 per cent grant lasted only until the end of 1980; from then there were annual decreases of 10 per cent until 1984 when the scheme was ended. Official statistics show that the government expenditure on New Bus Grants peaked, not surprisingly perhaps, in 1980/81 and tailed off to 1984.

Today's bus industry players are often accused of being subsidy-junkies, yet what its detractors often regard as subsidy is payment for services provided. Back in the 1970s, though…

# Standardisation
## –here now with the Daimler Fleetline

left: 30 ft. Fleetline double decker with front entrance.
below: 33 ft. Fleetline single decker with front entrance.

left: 30 ft. Fleetline double decker with central exit.
below: 33 ft. Fleetline single decker with central exit.

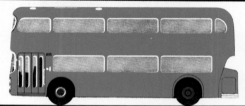

left: 33 ft. Fleetline double decker with front entrance.
below: 36 ft. Fleetline single decker with front entrance.

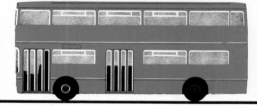

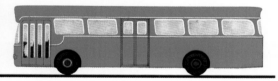

left: 33 ft. Fleetline double decker with central exit.
below: 36 ft. Fleetline single decker with central exit.

The advantages of Standardisation are obvious. Its introduction is another matter and, initially, could be very costly. **But not for Daimler Fleetline operators!**

The already well proven features of the Fleetline double decker have now been extended into single deck versions and offer the operator a complete range of vehicles for all types of operation, on one basic design of chassis with standardised running units.

Double deck chassis are available with 30ft. and 33ft. overall lengths and single deckers with 33ft. and 36ft. overall lengths.

Standardised running units include Gardner 6LX engines with 6LW and 6LXB alternatives; the Daimler epicyclic gearbox with right angle drive, and the dropped-centre drive axle.

And not only the main units are standard. Virtually all auxiliary

components are common to every Fleetline chassis, which will please your maintenance and stores staffs.

If you already operate Fleetlines, we invite you to consider the other variants available. If not, the introduction of Fleetlines could be a short step to Standardisation. Either way, let us send you full technical specifications.

**DAIMLER TRANSPORT VEHICLES LTD.,**
**COVENTRY, ENGLAND.**
**Daimler** Tel: Coventry 27626 (15 lines)

Daimler made a virtue of the standardisation offered by its single-deck and double-deck Fleetline models and illustrated this 1968 advert to show how the chassis met all of the New Bus Grants requirements, from 30ft-long single-door buses to longer single-door and dual-door versions.

*Above:* The New Bus Grants regulations were tweaked to cover models that did not exist in 1968, like the front-engined Volvo Ailsa. This is one of three experimental Ailsa/Alexander bought in 1975 by NBC and tested by its Maidstone & District subsidiary alongside Scania/MCW Metropolitans and standard Bristol VRT/ECWs.

*Right:* Standard New Bus Grants purchases for the National Bus Company fleets in the 1980s were the Bristol VRT double-decker and Leyland National single-decker, here represented by a 1979 Alder Valley VRT and a 1978 London Country B-series National.

# A Staggering Idea

Bus and coach operators have always looked to bodybuilders for ways of increasing the number of seats in their vehicles. More passengers obviously equates to more revenue and theoretically to more profit.

In the years before and after World War II luxury coaches typically had between 32 and 35 seats, all that was possible within the legal dimensions of the time. Double-deck coaches were one answer, but not one that operators really warmed to. But what about something in-between…?

Enter George Crellin, an experienced vehicle consultant, who wondered if tiered interlaced seating, brick-wall fashion, could be the answer. In a 27ft 6in-long coach this could increase seating to up to 60 passengers, it was claimed, surely something the coach companies would clamour for. It wasn't a brand-new idea, but was new to Britain and approval was gained in 1948 to use such vehicles.

In the Crellin-Duplex coach design, passengers sat in fours, with two facing pairs of seats. Roundly half the seats were at a slightly higher level, and the seats were staggered on both 'decks'. The overall height of 11ft 9in was more

One of two Crellin-Duplex bodies built by Lincs Trailers on AEC Regal III chassis in 1950 for Granville Tours, Grimsby.

Built by Mann Egerton in 1952 on underfloor-engined AEC Regal IV chassis, this Crellin-Duplex coach was supplied to Ripponden & District. Although it looks less ungainly than the front-engined Regal, it lacked the sleekness of the normal-height designs from other coachbuilders on the new breed of underfloor-engined single-deck chassis.

than a normal single-decker but 2ft lower than many lowbridge double-deckers.

Lincs Trailer of Scunthorpe built the first 11 Crellin-Duplex bodies. The very first was built in 1949 on Guy Arab III chassis, never a particularly popular choice for coaching work, and had seats for 46 (22/24). The next examples were built in 1950: three Foden PVFEs, two AEC Regal IIIs and two Leyland Tiger PS2/3s. A local operator, Granville Tours of Grimsby, bought the Regals and Tigers. Two of the Fodens went to Allenways, Birmingham, and the third to Parker, Lincoln. All seven were 43-seaters and the photo of one of the Regals shows the awkward and rather ungainly appearance.

How it was done. The original description reads: 'This dissected drawing shows the ingenious interior design, giving ample room for every passenger. Sociability is encouraged by seats arranged in facing pairs. Wide windows give splendid visibility with hedge-clear views from the half-deck seats.'

The final three Crellin-Duplex bodies built by Lincs Trailer appeared in 1951, all built to the newly authorised 30ft length, a change in regulations that would help to render the design obsolete. One was for use by passengers travelling to join KLM flights and was operated by United Service Transport, and the two others were Foden PVFEs for Ripponden & District.

Mann Egerton of Norwich took on the Crellin-Duplex patent and in 1952 built six of these coaches –

a re-bodied AEC Regent for Brunt's, Hatfield, three Crossley SD42s for Creamline, Borden, one AEC Regal IV for Ripponden & District, and one Leyland Royal Tiger for Homeland, Croydon. The last two were on underfloor-engined chassis and were 50-seaters. The same year Mann Egerton completed a part-built Foden PVFE for Sharp's, Manchester.

The design of the first Mann Egerton bodies owed much to the Lincs Trailer styling, but the last two Crellin-Duplex coaches were more modern and square cut – a Daimler Freeline for Don Everall, Wolverhampton, and a Foden PVRF (rear-engined) for Popular Coaches, London.

As conventional 30ft-long single-deck coaches on underfloor-engined chassis became more common, offering up to 41/43 seats, the awkward and claustrophobic Crellin-Duplex design fell out of favour.

Around the same time as George Crellin was developing his patent, O. V. S. Bulleid, chief mechanical engineer of Britain's Southern Railway, was developing his 4DD electric multiple-units, two of which ran in service with British Railways until 1971. Their layout was very similar to the Crellin-Duplex coaches, but more recent calls for double-deck trains in Britain, similar to those widely used in Europe, fell on deaf ears because of the tight British loading gauge.

Mann Egerton advertised what it described as a half-deck coach extensively in the trade press in the 1950s. This 1953 advert shows what turned out to be the last such coach built, on Foden's rear-engined PVRF chassis, and featuring the crisper body style carried by the last two bodies. It suggests that 20 men, their wives, girlfriends and children (50 in all) could fit into the coach with all their luggage too.

# Inappropriate Behaviour?

The way that buses and coaches and the products of their suppliers have been advertised over the years is worthy of a separate book, but it is sometimes shocking – and amusing too – to realise how the female form was used to brighten up the appeal of otherwise dull products and catch the eye of weary busmen.

The adverts featured here appeared in the 1950s and 1960s, when PC still stood for police constable or postcard rather than political correctness.

*Below and below right:* These Clayton Dewandre adverts for brakes probably brightened the life of many a bus engineer in 1962.

Clayton Dewandre's advertising agency presumably realised that bus brakes were difficult to illustrate effectively and so dreamt up a series of adverts featuring skimpily clad young ladies.

The respected paint manufacturer, T. & R. Williamson of Ripon decided that its products went on bus and coach bodies, so why not headline an advert 'Beautiful Bodies' and illustrate it with a young lady in a diaphanous dress. Some of the copy is amusing to read: 'Transport, like beautiful girls, has an image and reputation to maintain and, like the female of the species, it must withstand the closest inspection and stand up to the weathering of time.' Not, perhaps, a line that would be found in a 21st century advert.

Hallam, Sleigh & Cheston decided to feature a young lady in a short dress to sell its Silhouette driver's seat, under the headline 'The seat with everything a driver requires…' – though it is not clear if the young lady is the driver or the object of desire.

The favourite, though, is the line drawing of a lady wearing what appear to be hot pants before their time, to promote The Continental Super Luxury Coach Seat, manufactured by Rowland Hartrick Ltd of Birmingham but better known – really – as Lush Seating.

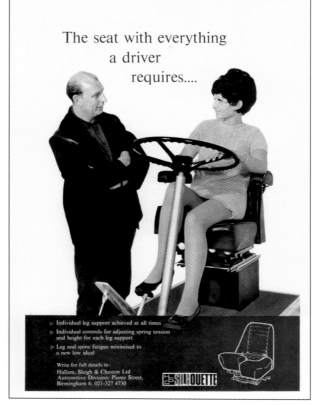

*Above:* Williamson's ad for Ripcerol was still very sexist, though more subtly so in this 1967 advert for paint.

*Above right:* The young lady with her foot hovering above the brake pedal in this 1968 advert for the Silhouette driver's seat looks as if she would know exactly where to stop.

*Right:* Possibly one of the more positive incentives to travel by coach, a detail from a 1950 advert for – wait for it – Lush Seating.

# And finally...

Official photographs of buses, taken by manufacturers and operators, have provided a rich source of information for transport historians. Completed buses were proudly posed in some suitable (and unsuitable) places over the years while the local commercial photographer came along with his equipment. Sometimes buses were posed outside the factory (Alexander, Roe), a good way to get the company name into the picture. Often quiet tree-lined roads were used (Leyland, Weymann and several others), while Metro-Cammell posed its buses in what appeared to be the middle of a grass-covered meadow, and East Lancs and Harrington appeared to take them along to the local public park. AEC, it should be said, actually got photographs of buses in service – or at least looking as if they were in service – and that is what today's official photos often try to do.

The problems arise when you get people involved. Hand-shaking handover shots are old hat, and sometimes the PR person or an imaginative photographer will aim to produce something a bit more interesting. On page 64 we see a transport minister struggling with an outsize flag that appears to be larger than the minibuses he is launching, and we close the book on these pages with some more of the unusual things people have been asked to do to promote buses, as well as a couple of examples where PR people and photographers have looked for something different.

Immaculately-dressed Mr. J. McKnight, general manager of Wigan Corporation Transport, studies what could well be a blank sheet of paper alongside a newly-delivered Northern Counties-bodied Leyland Royal Tiger in 1955. On the right is his rolling-stock superintendent.

*Above:* Just pretend you are ordinary bus passengers and hold it right there. The 1960 caption suggests that this Willowbrook-bodied AEC Reliance was being tested by officials at Aldenham Works before entering service, the main novelty here for London Transport being the two-door layout.

*Right:* Ireland's then Minister for Tourism, Seamus Brennan, is persuaded in 1990 to cut the tape to launch the first of the new Dublin Bus Leyland Olympian/Alexander fleet in O'Connell Street, watched by Dublin Bus, Alexander and Volvo personnel.

*Left:* When you are launching a new livery for Glasgow buses in 1996, why not persuade Elaine C. Smith, better known as Mary Doll in the Scottish 'Rab C. Nesbitt' TV sitcom, to come along and wield a paintbrush. The all-red scheme was never popular but would soon be replaced by First's corporate 'Barbie' livery.

*Left:* And finally... An official photo to confuse the historians in years to come. Two Volvo B7TL/Alexander ALX400, one Arriva, the other First, pose side by side on the East Leeds guided busway, although to achieve the required photo, the Arriva bus is facing the wrong way on the bi-directional busway. Just think of the opportunities for bus-racing...

# Further reading

These books were particularly useful while I was compiling this book, and readers will find more information on a range of subjects – blunders and otherwise – in them.

*ABC Buses and Coaches* by David J Warburton (1954), E. J. Smith (1956), Ian Allan Ltd

*Albion of Scotstoun* by Paul Adams and Roy Milligan, Albion Vehicle Preservation Trust, 1999

*Beyond Reality* by Doug Jack, Venture Publications, 1994

*Bristol RE – 40 years of service* by Duncan Roberts, NBC Books, 2002

*British Buses Since 1945* by Stephen Morris, Ian Allan Publishing Ltd, 1995

*Bus & Coach Recognition* by Alan Millar, Ian Allan Publishing Ltd, various editions

*Bus Review* by Stewart J Brown, Bus Enthusiast Publishing (annual issues published 1986-2001)

*CIE Buses 1945-1987* by Cyril McIntyre, Midland Publishing, 2004

*Characters of the Bus Industry* edited by Gavin Booth, The Omnibus Society, 2004

*Daimler* by Alan Townsin, Ian Allan Publishing Ltd, 2000

*London Transport and the Politicians* by Paul E. Garbutt, Ian Allan Ltd, 1985.

*Luxury Travel* by Stewart J. Brown, Capital Transport, 1998

*Municipal Buses in Colour 1959-1974* by Reg Wilson, Ian Allan Publishing, 1997

*Park Royal 1942-80* compiled by Alan Townsin, Transport Publishing Co 1980

*Routemaster Volume One 1954-1969* by Ken Blacker, Capital Transport, 1991

*Routemaster Volume Two 1970-1989* by Ken Blacker, Capital Transport, 1992

*The British Bus Today and Tomorrow* by Gavin Booth, Ian Allan Ltd 1983

*The Leyland Bus Mk2* by Doug Jack, Transport Publishing Co, 1984

*Transport Statistics Great Britain 1977-1987*, HMSO 1988

*80 Years of Guy Cars, Trucks and Buses* by Robin Hannay and Stuart Broach, Venture Publications Ltd, 1994